RAW FOOD

Anat Fritz

DK

CONTENTS

Breakfasts & SMOOTHIES

From a dollop of coconut yogurt on top of fresh "cheese" made with nuts, to raw food jam and smoothies, everything you need for a healthy breakfast can be found here. When a green smoothie is made of only fruit, greens, and water, it has an optimal detoxifying effect, so no additional sweetener is needed.

Salads, SNACKS & LUNCHES

Raw food encompasses much more than just salads. Wraps, breads, soups, stews, curries, and vegetable pasta—practically anything is possible. Many dishes can easily be made ahead of time for the following day's lunch. Expertly put together and nicely seasoned, choose from a variety of delicious dishes.

Desserts & CAKES

Healthy desserts offer adults and children alike a sensible alternative to sugary snacks. If something sweet is needed for dessert, it can be a piece of delicious cake or crumble, but a few spoonfuls of chia pudding or a little peanut butter ball covered in chocolate will also complete every meal.

WHY RAW?

Raw Food is designed to appeal to all those who are interested in raw food, whether they're already incorporating it into their diets or they're just needing a bit of guidance on how to include it in their daily menu. However, I don't tackle every aspect of the raw food debate. In this book, I deal with my own experiences and anything related to them that I deem important. I would like to share my knowledge of raw food as it has become a vital part of my life.

The term "raw food" applies to all food not heated over a certain temperature, commonly agreed to be 104°F (40°C). There are varying viewpoints on this, but this is the scientifically acknowledged "limit" above which heat-sensitive vitamins and enzymes in food are diminished or lost altogether—in other words, cooked away.

Actually, the topic is not all that complicated. One thing is for sure: eating raw food for a long time, a short time, occasionally, or even in a medicinal capacity is always beneficial. I've been a "raw vegan" (see Introduction, p.8) for more than 2 years now. Aside from the health benefits, following a raw food diet fairly strictly promotes a feeling of well-being and increases vitality and beauty. The positive effects can be seen after even just a short time. Your skin becomes smoother, your eyes brighter, and your mood also improves. Raw food even helps fight against depression. The term "superfood" says it all—it expresses how effective "raw food" really is.

I hope the recipes in this book inspire you, or even lead you, to add raw food to your daily diet. Every change starts with just one small first step!

Anat Fritz

INTRODUCTION

Vegetarian, vegan, or raw?

The decision to live as a raw vegan utterly changed my relationship to nutrition. Once I became a raw vegan, I truly felt the meaning of the principle "eat to live" and not "live to eat." In saying this, I am thinking primarily about consuming food that is still full of energy and abstaining from milk, meat, and products derived from animals. These are hard to digest and acidify the gut flora (the microorganisms in our intestines that help digest certain foods). Excessive consumption of these foods can increase the risk of chronic conditions such as high cholesterol levels, which can result in heart disease and stroke.

The transition from vegetarian to vegan to raw food cuisine is easy to explain. Vegetarians abstain from eating foods produced by killing animals, but their diets include products derived from animals, such as milk, cheese, and honey. On the other hand, vegans do not eat any animal foods whatsoever, not even foods processed using animal products. The next step from vegan to raw food cuisine is fairly straightforward.

Both vegan and raw food cuisines are completely cholesterol-free since both refrain from using animal products. Both use every available kind of fruit and vegetable, many greens and herbs, seeds, and nuts but also sprouts, seaweed, and natural flavorings. Vegan cuisine also uses soy products. Because they are heated, and difficult to digest, soy products do not play a role in raw food cuisine.

RAW FOOD IS RICH IN NUTRIENTS AND ENZYMES

When we think about "heat," we arrive at the very heart of raw food. It is key to raw food cuisine that no ingredient, neither in its production nor in its processing, is heated above a certain temperature. The reason is that the enzymes, vitamins, and mineral nutrients that are diminished or utterly lost when food is cooked remain intact when food is not cooked. The temperature limit for raw food cuisine is about 104°F (40°C). I say "about" because there are varying viewpoints about and approaches to this guideline. Some raw food cooks don't heat food beyond 98.6°F (37°C), while others heat food to 107.6°F (42°C) or 109.4°F (43°C). In this book, we sit in the middle of this range at 104°F (40°C).

Enzymes are essential to healthy digestion. I once heard an appropriate saying: "You are not what you eat, but what you digest!" In my experience, it is not just what kinds of foods you consume that are important, but how they are digested is at least as important as nutrition for the promotion of good health and the prevention of illness.

Raw foods, especially green smoothies, are wonderful for promoting digestion and detoxifying the body. Along with their obvious detoxifying effect, raw foods help on an entirely different level. I often hear from people who eat "normal" cooked food that they no longer know which foods are beneficial to them and which ones are better to avoid.

Eating a raw food diet gives you clarity, reawakening you to your own perceptions. Why? By renouncing additives, sugar, and other similar ingredients that are hard for the body to process, your system cleanses itself from the inside out, giving you an "unfiltered" feeling and awareness of what is and isn't good for your body. It gives you back an original sense of what you need to eat. I find this very important. There is such a huge number and astonishing variety of industrially processed foods, making it hard to discern what exactly it is that your body needs.

EATING WITH AWARENESS

I don't generally care much for dogma and fanaticism, either generally or in the culinary realm. With this book, I am not trying to convert people into 100 percent raw food eaters, since I hope that the recipes will be convincing enough without any underlying ideology.

For example, although I have been a raw food eater for more than 2 years, I still toast my sesame seeds since I love their aroma so much that I could not do without them.

When I have guests over, I can easily get around serving cooked food, but you can be slightly flexible. When I went to my first Thanksgiving dinner, I refrained from showing up with my own container of food. Instead, I brought along a raw food key lime pie and enjoyed the vegetable sides. The next day, I returned to my green smoothie and right away could feel why I prefer eating raw food.

I am also happy to use sweeteners. I still eat honey—a taboo for hard-core vegans and raw food eaters since it is produced by animals. When thinking about sweeteners, it is more important to move away from industrially processed sugar toward alternative sweeteners, such as dates and high-quality maple syrup, as well as honey, of course. Agave syrup is listed in many recipes in this book for the benefit of vegans, although according to new research, this is not healthier than sugar.

Cooking without foods derived from animals is not imperative for me but is a path to healthier nutrition and is good for our bodies as well as our minds. We should all find our "inner nutritional centers" and develop our own principles, ones that certainly can be broken occasionally—as I do myself.

Switching from cooked to raw food is worthwhile, even if you do so only sporadically. For, as you will learn from my recipes, raw food also leads to entirely new taste discoveries.

 **TIP** Many sweeteners and seasonings serve as alternatives to sugar and salt and play a large role in raw food cuisine. On page 150, you will find information about various ingredients used in raw food cuisine that might, at first, seem unusual to you.

Breakfasts & SMOOTHIES

BREAKFAST ★

Start your day with energy

Breakfast is considered to be the most important meal of the day. It is supposed to provide us with enough energy to give us a good and healthy start to the day. When I ate what I used to consider a normal breakfast, I always wanted to go back to bed immediately and sleep, giving me a chance to digest my food. Okay, I admit I am exaggerating just a bit ... but for me, a breakfast must give one energy, instead of stealing energy. In my experience, a breakfast consisting of scrambled eggs, sausage, and bread with jam belongs more to the latter category.

Apart from smoothies, I usually prepare my breakfast foods the evening before, or even earlier. In the morning, I want to be able just to open the fridge and take out whatever I feel like eating. Most of my breakfast foods taste even better when they have soaked, marinated, or stood overnight. Try it out!

COCONUT MILK INSTEAD OF COW'S MILK

Before my raw vegan period, I was a big fan of dairy products. Probiotic yogurt made from young coconut (see p.25) is both a fantastic and disproportionately healthier alternative. It promotes healthy gut flora and has a well-known positive effect—one tablespoon in the morning, one at midday, and one in the evening will help immeasurably to keep that sweet tooth in check. While it is true that hunting for young coconut can be a bit time-consuming, it is really worth it for this recipe. I enjoy this yogurt most of all on its own so I can savor the delicate coconut flavor. But, of course, you also can stir in muesli and/or fresh fruit.

SMOOTHIES MAKE YOU HAPPY

Everything that you need for a constructive, happy start to the day can be put in a smoothie. A smoothie enlivens the spirits and quenches the first hunger pangs. Try it out for a while. For this reason, I've devoted a bit more room to the smoothie recipes in the breakfast chapter. As far as types of smoothies go, my favorite is the green smoothie. Its positive effect is surely worth dedicating pages to, if not an entire book.

I would like to provide just a bit of information for the raw food beginner. Drinking blended fruit and salad greens provides the body with many important and necessary vitamins, enzymes, and mineral nutrients. Including green smoothies in your daily life is an easy way to increase the amount of "greenery" in your diet. Go ahead and experiment with baby spinach, mâche, or arugula. Baby spinach makes a smoothie thicker. Mâche does not have much flavor, but it has a higher nutritional value than Boston lettuce. Arugula provides a bit of tartness. It is best to use arugula with two more neutral-tasting greens.

The chlorophyll factor

The chlorophyll factor is a good reason to always choose a green smoothie over a fruit smoothie! The chlorophyll contained in green vegetables is a powerful source of vitality. We all know that chlorophyll makes it possible for plants to photosynthesize and that plants grow and thrive because of this process. In humans, the chlorophyll in green smoothies works to detoxify the body, because it helps the body build new blood cells.

BUCKWHEAT OATMEAL

Serves 2–3 ▪ Preparation time: 10–15 minutes plus soaking

Soaked buckwheat groats make an excellent breakfast oatmeal. They taste even better if you soak them in juice, since this gives them a sweet flavor. Making this oatmeal with freshly squeezed orange juice is my favorite version, but it is also fantastic made with prune juice.

½ cup raw buckwheat groats

⅔ cup fresh orange juice

1 apple

⅔ cup almond milk (see p.148) or almond cream (see p.143)

3 tbsp chia seeds

1 tsp white sesame seeds (optional)

pinch of ground cinnamon

honey or maple syrup, to taste

chopped walnuts, to taste

1 Put the buckwheat groats and the orange juice into a bowl. Allow to soak in the refrigerator overnight. Just before using them, drain and rinse the buckwheat.

2 Cut the apple into quarters and place into a blender, along with the almond milk or almond cream. Purée briefly on a low setting so that the mixture does not liquify too much. Transfer the mixture to a large bowl, add the chia seeds and the soaked buckwheat, and mix everything together to combine. If using the sesame seeds (see p.10), place them in a frying pan and toast them slightly without using any oil.

3 Sprinkle the sesame seeds and cinnamon over the buckwheat. Add honey or maple syrup and walnuts, to taste.

TIP

The buckwheat oatmeal in this recipe is so flavorful and filling that you really don't need to add anything else to it. However, if you have a hankering for a bit of fruitiness, add a few blueberries or dried fruit of your choice. Vegans who abstain from honey can sweeten the oatmeal with maple syrup.

EXOTIC FRUIT SNACK

Makes 2 dehydrating trays ▪ Preparation time: 30 minutes plus dehydration

When I make this recipe, I sometimes vary the dehydrating time, which makes a huge difference (see tip). However, it's important that the pieces don't become too dry and that they can still be easily chewed.

For the marinade:

a few sprigs thyme

3–4 tbsp tamari or dark soy sauce

1 tsp cold-pressed sesame oil

pinch of cayenne pepper

For the vegetables and fruit:

1 tomato

½ eggplant

½ sweet potato

1 carrot

½ mango

1 apple

You will also need:

2 dehydrating trays

food dehydrator

1 To make the marinade, pick the thyme leaves and chop them finely. In a large bowl, combine the tamari or soy sauce, sesame oil, thyme, and cayenne pepper.

2 Remove the green stem from the tomato and cut it into thick slices. Peel the eggplant, sweet potato, and carrot. Cut the eggplant horizontally into slices. Cut the sweet potato lengthwise in half and slice into half-moon-shaped pieces. Slice the carrot lengthwise into strips. Peel the mango, cut the flesh off the pit, and finely slice it lengthwise into strips. Cut the apple in half, remove the core, and cut into half-moon-shaped pieces.

3 Put the pieces of fruit and vegetables into the bowl containing the marinade, and toss gently to combine. Spread out the pieces evenly on the dehydrating trays, and put in the food dehydrator to dry for 7–9 hours at 104°F (40°C).

TIP The dried fruit and vegetables keep best when they are stored in a plastic container. The longer they have been dried, the longer they will keep, but the harder they will be. You should eat them within 1–2 weeks.

APRICOT & ROSEMARY *jam*

Makes 1 jar ▪ Preparation time: 20 minutes plus soaking

This jam enhances ice cream and muesli, but the classic way of serving it—on crackers or sandwich bread—is my favorite! I like apricot and rosemary jam when it still has pieces of fruit in it, which is why when I make it, the jam is relatively coarse.

2 cups dried apricots
sprig of rosemary
½ lemon
1–1½ tbsp agave syrup

1 Place the apricots in a bowl and add enough water just to cover them. Put a plate on top of the bowl and soak overnight in the refrigerator. Before using the apricots, drain them over a bowl and reserve the liquid (see tip).

2 Using a large knife, coarsely chop the apricots. Then, mash them with a fork until they have a jamlike consistency.

3 Pick the rosemary leaves, and chop them finely. Juice the lemon. Stir the rosemary, lemon juice, and agave syrup into the mashed apricots. Spoon the jam into a jar with a screw-top lid and seal tightly. If you always use a clean spoon each time you take out a portion, the jam will keep in the fridge for 4–5 days.

TIP Apricot soaking water makes a good sweetener for juices and smoothies, so always save the liquid when you drain the fruit. For an exotic taste, add 1 tablespoon of freshly pressed mandarin juice to the jam. The flavor of mandarin goes very well with the apricot and lemon mixture.

* PLUM &
CARDAMOM
jam

Makes 2 jars ▪ Preparation time: 20 minutes plus soaking and chilling

This plum jam recipe is ideal if you do not have a food dehydrator but would still like to savor a sweet spread. It is delicious slathered on crackers and sandwich bread, added to muesli, or used in desserts.

4 tbsp white chia seeds
½ cup apple juice (optional)
1lb 2oz (500g) plums
1 tsp ground cinnamon
pinch of ground cardamom
drop of vanilla extract
1 tbsp lemon juice
3 tbsp honey or agave syrup

1 Soak the chia seeds in the apple juice, or use water, for 15 minutes. In the meantime, pit the plums.

2 Place the plums, cinnamon, cardamom, vanilla extract, lemon juice, and honey or agave into a blender and process on the lowest setting. Make sure you can see little pieces of plum in the mixture and that it does not become too runny. Add the chia seeds, and process again briefly.

3 Spoon the plum jam into jars with screw-top lids. Put the jars in the refrigerator, and let sit for at least 1 hour. The swollen chia seeds will further thicken the mixture. If you always use a clean spoon each time you take out a portion, the jam will keep in the refrigerator for 4–5 days.

PROBIOTIC COCONUT *yogurt*

Makes 1 jar ▪ Preparation time: 20 minutes plus soaking

In my opinion, one of the most impressive raw food discoveries was, and still is, raw vegan yogurt—a small alchemic miracle that is made from just two ingredients: coconut and kefir starter culture. Since kefir starter consists of probiotic bacteria, it is not, strictly speaking, a vegan ingredient.

2–3 young coconuts

1 packet of kefir starter culture

1 Using a large, heavy knife, hack around the pointed ends of the coconuts and break off the lids. Pour the coconut water into a measuring cup, measuring 2 cups. Save any extra coconut water to use in another recipe.

2 Using a tablespoon, scrape the soft coconut meat from the inside shells and set aside. Pour the coconut water through a fine-meshed sieve into a pan. Slowly heat the water over low to medium heat until it is lukewarm. Add the kefir starter culture, and, using a wire whisk, mix everything together well.

3 Place the coconut meat and coconut water into a blender or food processor, and purée.

4 Pour the mixture into a jar that has been sterilized with boiling water. Cover it with a towel, and leave the mixture in a warm place for at least 24 hours. The longer the now tart-tasting yogurt rests, the tarter and firmer it will be. Stir well once then refrigerate. Kept cold, it will keep for about 1 week.

TIP Young coconuts are coconuts that are picked when they are still green, and then the husk is removed. You can purchase young coconuts (see photo) in Asian grocery stores and online.

I like to experiment with cheeselike flavors, since, I must admit, I sometimes miss my beloved dairy products. In this recipe, the cashew "cheese" comes close to the taste of cream cheese. The spread is also a treat served on its own with bread and crackers.

* *Oregano* CASHEW CHEESE BALLS

Serves 2–3 ▪ Preparation time cashew "cream cheese": 15 minutes plus soaking and chilling ▪ Preparation time cheese balls: 10 minutes plus chilling

For the cashew "cream cheese":

1 cup unsalted cashews

2 scallions

1 garlic clove

3–4 sprigs oregano

4–5 tbsp lemon juice

1 tsp onion powder (see p.152)

2 tbsp nutritional yeast

pinch of Fleur de Sel

For the balls:

4–5 Brussels sprouts

2 tbsp white sesame seeds (optional)

1 Cover the cashews with cold water and soak overnight.

2 Pour the nuts into a sieve and let drain. Slice the scallions into thin rings. Peel the garlic. Pick and chop the oregano leaves.

3 Place all the ingredients, except for the onion powder and oregano, into a blender. Process until thick and creamy. If the ingredients are very hard to blend, add a bit of water, as needed.

4 Transfer the mixture to a bowl. Stir in the onion powder and the oregano. Cover the bowl with plastic wrap, and refrigerate for at least 1 hour, or until firm.

5 Remove the outer leaves from the Brussels sprouts. Using a grater or knife, shred the sprouts finely. (If you use a food processor, they will be shredded too finely.) Add the shredded sprouts to the cashew mixture, and combine well. Form the mixture into bite-size balls. To ensure that the balls are easy to form, don't add all the shredded Brussels sprouts in one go. If using sesame seeds (see p.10), place them in a frying pan without any fat, and toast them until they are golden brown.

6 Roll the balls in the sesame seeds and place them side by side in a shallow dish. Cover with plastic wrap, and refrigerate for 1 hour, or until they are firm.

TIP The taste reminds me of falafel. Instead of oregano, other herbs, such as basil or marjoram, can be used. The recipe isn't 100 percent vegan because it calls for nutritional yeast. This does, however, provide a lot of flavor.

CRISPBREAD

**Makes 3–4 dehydrating trays ▪ Preparation time:
40 minutes plus dehydration**

This very simple recipe is suitable for beginners, as long as you follow one basic rule: if the raw mixture tastes good before it is dehydrated, then the end result will also taste good, so always do a taste test before you dehydrate the mixture! The only change caused by the dehydration process is that the flavor becomes more intense.

5 carrots

**1 small zucchini
(about 3oz/80g)**

2 garlic cloves

**1 cup almond pulp
(see tip, p.45 and p.143)**

3½ tbsp ground flaxseed

1 tsp mild curry powder

**salt and freshly ground
black pepper**

You will also need:

3–4 dehydrating trays

food dehydrator

1 Peel the carrots, and then cut the carrots and zucchini into large pieces. Peel the garlic and squeeze it through a garlic press.

2 Place the carrots, zucchini, and garlic into a food processor and purée until smooth. Add the almond pulp, ground flaxseed, and curry powder. Using a kitchen spoon or wire whisk, combine all the ingredients well, making sure that there are no lumps. Season to taste.

3 Spread the mixture on the dehydrating trays ¼in (5mm) thick. Dry in the food dehydrator for 4–5 hours at 104°F (40°C). After the time is up, test to see whether the crispbread is hard enough to turn over. If it is not, dry it for ½–1 hour more. Test the crispbread again, turn it over, and leave it on the trays to dry completely. Before serving, carefully break the crispbread into large pieces.

Green delight

Makes 1 glass ▪ Preparation time: 5 minutes

My friend Katharina invented this smoothie. It was one of her first creations after I persuaded her to try these vitamin bombs. For, at heart, she is a passionate champion of her Polish (meat) cuisine.

¼ **honeydew melon**
¼ **avocado**
large handful of mâche
squeeze of lemon juice
1 tbsp raisins
drop of vanilla extract

Seed the melon. Slice the avocado lengthwise in half, remove the pit, and scoop out the avocado flesh. Place the avocado, mâche, lemon juice, raisins, and vanilla extract into a blender. Add ⅔ cup water and purée until smooth.

VITAMIN BOMB

Makes 1–2 glasses ▪ Preparation time: 5 minutes

handful of young kale
⅔ **cup unsweetened**
  coconut water
1 banana
handful of fresh or frozen
  raspberries
1 tsp maca powder (see p.152)

Place all the ingredients into a blender, and purée until smooth. If needed, add a little water.

Kale turns every dish into a tasty source of vitamins and is becoming very popular, available now year-round in North America. In this recipe, you can substitute frozen for fresh raspberries.

SUMMER LOVE

Makes 1 glass ▪ Preparation time: 5 minutes

From any standpoint, this is a super smoothie. Dandelion has a cleansing effect, making it good for the kidneys and liver. Mandarin oranges and grapefruit are a wonderful combination and refreshing good mood fruits!

2 mandarin oranges
1 grapefruit
¼ **banana**
small handful of dandelion
  greens
handful of baby spinach
4 ice cubes
1 tbsp honey or agave syrup

Peel and slice the oranges, grapefruit, and banana. Place all the ingredients into a blender and purée on the highest setting until smooth. If needed, you can add a bit of water so the ingredients purée better. Serve the smoothie well chilled.

PERSIMMON SPINACH *smoothie*

Serves 2 ▪ Preparation time: 10 minutes

If you blend all the ingredients for this smoothie together, you are likely to end up with a brownish-colored drink. While this doesn't affect the taste in the least, it might bring to mind the well-known saying, "You eat with your eyes first." Fortunately, I remembered the layered desserts of the 1980s, popular with adults and children alike. In this smoothie, the fruits and vegetables are puréed separately and then poured in two layers for a genuine '80s retro look!

2 ripe persimmons
½ ripe mango
½ lime
handful of white grapes (seedless)
6⅔ cups baby spinach
2–3 fresh mint leaves
pinch of cayenne pepper

1 Cut the stems off the persimmons and slice the persimmons into large pieces. Peel the mango, and cut the mango flesh off the pit.

2 Juice the lime. Place the persimmons, mango, and lime juice into a blender and purée on the highest setting for about 30 seconds. Pour out equal amounts of the persimmon and mango mixture into two glasses.

3 Put the grapes, spinach, mint, cayenne pepper, and ⅔ cup water into a blender. Purée on the highest setting for about 30 seconds. Carefully pour out equal amounts of the puréed grape and spinach mixture on top of the first layers of fruit, and serve.

TIP Persimmon thickens fairly quickly, so if you want to be able to drink it easily, it is best to serve this smoothie immediately. You can also eat it later.

In no time, this smoothie can be transformed into a tangy granita—a welcome refreshment on a hot summer's day. This recipe doesn't need any additional sweeteners or extra water. I prefer to spoon the smoothie out of the glass, with utmost pleasure!

* GRAPEFRUIT *smoothie*

Makes 2 glasses ▪ Preparation time: 5 minutes plus freezing

3 pink grapefruit
1–1½ tsp fresh rosemary
5–6 ice cubes

Peel and segment the grapefruit then place in blender with the rosemary and ice cubes. Purée until smooth.

Test to see whether the drink is liquid enough. If not, add water in small batches as needed. Either drink the smoothie right away or turn it into a granita. To do this, pour the smoothie into a shallow bowl and place in the freezer for about 2 hours, stirring occasionally with a fork.

* PINEAPPLE & MINT *smoothie*

Makes 2 glasses ▪ Preparation time: 5 minutes plus chilling or freezing

½ ripe pineapple
7–8 mint leaves, plus a few extra, to decorate
5–6 ice cubes

Peel, core, and slice the pineapple. Place the pineapple, mint leaves, and ice cubes into a blender, and purée on the highest setting for 30 seconds. Serve chilled, or freeze the mixture and turn it into a granita (see recipe, above).

Just like grapefruit, pineapple is a great ingredient for making refreshing drinks. It is also low in calories and rich in minerals and vitamins. Pineapple is not suitable for diet drinks, though, since its relatively high fructose content triggers feelings of hunger. The mint balances the sweetness of the pineapple and gives the smoothie a refreshing flavor.

If you have a juicer that can extract the juice from greens, then this smoothie, in terms of both taste and health, is the ultimate for vitality! It purges and is also chock-full of vitamins. It's a great wake-up drink in the morning!

✳ GREEN WONDER *smoothie*

Makes 1 large glass ▪ Preparation time: 10 minutes

½ peach
½ cup orange juice
1 cup celery juice
2 tbsp lime juice
1 tsp cilantro juice
1 tsp parsley juice
pinch of Himalayan salt
2–3 ice cubes

Remove the pit from the peach and slice in half. Place the peach, the squeezed juices, salt, and ice cubes into a blender. Purée until smooth.

JUICY LUCY DETOX *juice*

Makes 1–2 glasses ▪ Preparation time: 10 minutes

1¼ cups pineapple
½ sweet apple
½ lime
1 small piece (½in/1cm) fresh ginger
1 celery stick, including the leaves
1 handful of mâche or baby spinach

1 piece (2in/5cm) cucumber
1 pinch of ground cayenne pepper
1 tsp spirulina powder

Peel, core, and slice the pineapple, and core and slice the apple. Juice the lime, and peel the ginger. Place all the ingredients into a blender and add 1 cup water. Purée until smooth. Set a fine-meshed sieve over a bowl, and push the mixture through the sieve so that only liquid ends up in the bowl.

1 pear

1 banana

4 cups mâche

½ cup unsweetened coconut water, or water

drop of vanilla extract

BIBA ⭐

Makes 1 glass ▪ Preparation time: 5 minutes

Cut the pear into quarters and remove the core. Peel the banana. Place all the ingredients into a blender, and purée until smooth.

½ banana

1 mango

½ lime

1 tbsp maca powder (see p.152)

large handful of mâche or baby spinach

1 piece (2¾in/7cm) cucumber

½ cup unsweetened coconut water, or water

ice cubes, to taste

SWEET MONDAY

Makes 1 large glass ▪ Preparation time: 5 minutes

Peel the banana and mango, and cut the mango flesh off the pit. Juice the lime. Place all the ingredients into a blender, and purée until smooth. If the smoothie is too thick, add a bit more water.

1 pear

1 banana

4 cups mâche

½ cup unsweetened coconut water, or water

drop of vanilla extract

B12-Booster ⭐

Makes 1 glass ▪ Preparation time: 5 minutes

Cut the pear into quarters and remove the core. Peel the banana. Place all the ingredients into a blender, and purée until smooth.

½ banana

1 mandarin orange

½ ripe mango

2 handfuls romaine lettuce

1 piece (2¾in/7cm) cucumber

2–3 ice cubes

1 cup unsweetened coconut water, or water

BAMAMA

Makes 1–2 glasses ▪ Preparation time: 5 minutes

Peel the banana, mandarin orange, and mango. Cut the mango flesh off the pit and slice the orange. Place all the ingredients into a blender. Start to process the ingredients on a low setting, and then increase the speed bit by bit until the mixture is thick and creamy.

If you are able to buy young coconut meat (and more and more online retailers are offering young coconut), then it is worth doing so to try out this recipe. This is, for me, more of a dessert than a drink, but of course it still counts as a smoothie.

SOFT DREAM

Makes 2 glasses ▪ Preparation time: 10 minutes

1 mango
1 young coconut
1–2 tsp coconut sugar
small handful of fresh mint leaves or 2 drops mint oil

1 Peel the mango and cut the mango flesh off the pit.

2 Using a large, heavy knife, hack around the pointed end of the coconut and break off the lid. Pour the coconut water into a measuring cup, measuring out ⅔–¾ cup. Save the extra liquid to use in another recipe.

3 Using a tablespoon, scrape the coconut meat from the inside shell and set aside. Sieve the coconut water through a fine-meshed sieve.

4 Place all the ingredients into a blender. Purée until smooth.

LUSCIOUS LASSI

Makes 2 glasses ▪ Preparation time: 10 minutes plus chilling

1 cup almond milk (see p.148)
3 tbsp carrot juice
2 tbsp agave syrup
½ tsp ground cardamom seeds
pinch of grated turmeric root
1 tsp rose water

Place all the ingredients into a blender. Purée on the highest setting for 1 minute. Chill the lassi in the refrigerator for 30 minutes before serving.

This drink was developed by Linas Kesminas, a good friend of mine. He is an exceptionally gifted raw food chef, and I have learned many of my tips and tricks from him. The extraordinary, delectable taste of this drink took me by surprise—yet it is so easy to make, it had to have a place in our collection of recipes.

RAWNOLA

Serves 10 ▪ Preparation time: 40 minutes plus soaking and dehydration

This recipe, just one of countless muesli variations, is terrific and so simple to make! It's delicious served with almond milk. You can also prepare it with any other kind of nut milk (I love tiger nut milk). I prefer rawnola with fresh blueberries, banana, and orange juice, but here, you can exercise boundless creativity. Now, onward!

1 cup raw buckwheat groats

1 cup sunflower seeds

3 apples

1¼ cups walnuts

⅓ cup pumpkin seeds

1 cup raisins

½ cup shredded coconut

¼ cup poppy seeds

3 tbsp sesame seeds

zest of 1 organic orange

¼ tsp grated nutmeg

3 tbsp ground cinnamon

1 tsp vanilla extract

pinch of salt

1 cup orange juice

You will also need:
3–4 dehydrating trays
food dehydrator

1 Soak the buckwheat groats and the sunflower seeds overnight. Place in a sieve, and rinse under cold running water. Lay them out on paper towels to drain.

2 Cut the apples into quarters and remove the cores. Place the pieces of apple, the walnuts, and the pumpkin seeds into a food processor and chop them coarsely. Pour the mixture into a bowl. Using your hand, mix in the remaining ingredients apart from the orange juice. Pour the orange juice into the bowl, and allow the mixture to soak for about 30 minutes.

3 Spread out the mixture on the dehydrating trays. Put the trays into the food dehydrator. Drying times vary, but, dried at 104°F (40°C), the muesli will usually take between 7 and 8 hours to dry. Once dry, break up the larger clumps, as needed.

TIP

Stir raw cacao nibs and grated apple into the mixture. This recipe makes a large quantity, since the muesli will keep for at least 1 week in an airtight container. I always like to err on the side of caution when dehydrating the mixture, since I like my muesli to be dry—to ensure that it keeps longer and is nice and crunchy, dry it overnight for 10 hours.

TIGER NUT COCOA

Makes 3–4 glasses ▪ Preparation time: 10 minutes plus soaking

2 cups tiger nuts
1 tbsp raw cocoa powder
4 dates
pinch of salt

You will also need:
nut milk bag

TIP The tiger nut pulp remaining in the bag can be frozen or kept in the fridge. You can use it to make other delicious dishes, such as desserts or breakfast muesli.

1 Put the tiger nuts in a bowl, cover with cold water, and let them soak overnight. Just before using the nuts, rinse and drain them.

2 Place the tiger nuts into a blender. Add 4¼ cups water, and purée. Pour the mixture into a nut milk bag. Using your hands, squeeze out the liquid.

3 Return the nut milk to the blender. Add the cocoa, the pitted dates, and the salt. Purée the ingredients thoroughly.

This drink tastes every bit as good as regular cocoa. If tiger nuts are not available, you can use any kind of nut you like. Tiger nuts are, in fact, not nuts, but root vegetables, making this safe for people with nut allergies. It is also ideal for people who are lactose intolerant! If you wish to drink it warm, simply let the blender run longer—a good trick for warming up food and drinks, and which doesn't spoil the taste.

Nut milk treat

Makes 3–4 glasses ▪ Preparation time: 10 minutes plus soaking

1 recipe almond milk (see p.148)
2 dates
1 tsp chia seeds
1 tbsp honey or agave syrup
1 tsp lucuma powder
1–2 tsp maca powder
1 tbsp raw cocoa powder
drop of vanilla extract
½ tsp ground cinnamon
pinch of salt

You will also need:
nut milk bag

1 Prepare the almond milk. Pit the dates.

2 Place all the ingredients into a blender and purée until thoroughly mixed. If you blend it for long enough, the drink will be nice and foamy—yummy!

This version is the Rolls-Royce of raw-vegan milk drinks. The sweet and creamy milk is a real treat on cold days, or just simply when you really need something sweet.

TIP This drink keeps well in the fridge for about 2 days, if you can resist gulping it down immediately. I prefer to use honey in it rather than agave syrup.

Salads, Snacks & Lunches

LUNCH

Charge your battery instead of slowing down your day

Contrary to general opinion, lunch in raw food cuisine is filling and varied. Due to the fresh, enzyme-rich nutrients in the ingredients used, the dishes are rich and, despite this (or perhaps because of it), easy to digest. The difference between a raw food lunch and a regular lunch—unless the latter consists of a fresh salad—is that, after a raw food lunch, you can resume your day fresh and full of energy. The midday meal doesn't lie heavily in your stomach, feel hard to digest, and make you long for a rest, if not a nap.

GOOD PREPARATION IS HALF THE WORK

In choosing recipes for this book, I made sure that the dishes really could be made quickly. Of course, some do call for dried ingredients, and you will need to use a food dehydrator first or soak the ingredients ahead of time. While this can seem an interminable process, all you need to do is plan ahead a bit. Luckily, dehydration makes food keep longer—so you can simply make a large quantity from the start. And soaking nuts overnight takes little effort. What sounds a bit inconvenient at first is really just a question of getting used to doing something. The actual preparation time of the recipes—even those using dehydrated ingredients or those that need to be soaked in advance—generally passes very quickly.

Sauces—the secret of flavor

When I have a bit of free time, I like to prepare a variety of sauces that will keep well in the fridge for a few days. In this way, I can decide at lunchtime what I feel like eating, without having to limit myself or spend a lot of time preparing. With a spiralizer and a bit of practice, vegetable spaghetti is ready in a jiffy. Then, I just add the sauce of my choice, and the meal is ready! It is very uncomplicated to make. Having a few good sauces on hand is, in general, very helpful when preparing raw food dishes. They are more or less the secret of the flavor, allowing you to create different tastes even when using similar ingredients. And, of course, double portions can be prepared or the leftovers kept in the fridge for the next day.

MORE QUALITY OF LIFE THANKS TO RAW FOOD

A good and well-balanced lunch usually keeps you from feeling hungry until early evening. For our body, this is exactly the right timing, as you should avoid having to digest a complete meal after about 7 p.m. If you are well organized, you can bring containers full of ready-prepared snacks to work. For my part, I rely on the fact that today there are many organic-food stores and even fruit stalls where I can quickly buy an apple or a box of blueberries. And when I go out to eat, I know that salads are offered everywhere now. My day-to-day life definitely has gained in quality since I became a raw food eater, which to me is the primary reason and goal of my raw food diet.

Banana & LETTUCE WRAP

Serves 1 ▪ Preparation time: 5 minutes

I have included this very simple "recipe" that is absurdly easy to prepare since, every time I prepare it, I see pleasantly surprised faces. And then, afterward, I have caught my friends "banana wrapping!"

1 large ripe banana

pinch of ground cinnamon

1 leaf romaine lettuce

cacao nibs, to taste

You will also need:

toothpicks

1 Peel the banana, sprinkle it with cinnamon, and wrap it in the salad leaf.

2 Either eat the banana-lettuce wrap whole or cut it into bite-size pieces. Secure each piece with a toothpick and arrange the pieces on a plate. If desired, sprinkle the pieces with 1 tablespoon of cacao nibs.

TIP For a variation, spread 1 tablespoon of your favorite nut butter, almond paste (see p.148), or coconut cream on the banana. This is really very filling. I like the lighter version better—and the scales like it, too!

Marinated WATERMELON

Serves 4 ▪ Preparation time: 5 minutes plus chilling

This is a magical little dish that makes a huge impression on guests. Served in small shallow dishes, the 3–4 pieces of watermelon have something a bit Zen-like about them, which is why this recipe could also be called "Zen on a plate."

⅛ **watermelon**

3–4 basil leaves

2 tbsp balsamic vinegar

pinch of salt

1 Cut out the watermelon flesh from the shell, remove the seeds, and slice into bite-size cubes. Slice the basil leaves into thin strips.

2 Put the cubes of melon into a bowl. Add the balsamic vinegar and basil, and combine very carefully so that the watermelon cubes remain intact. Season to taste with a bit of salt, and let stand for a few minutes. Put the dish into the refrigerator to chill for at least 1 hour before serving.

3 Divide the melon cubes between small shallow bowls or plates, and serve as an appetizer.

VEGETABLE
STEW

Serves 3–4 ▪ Preparation time: 30 minutes plus soaking

This stew is especially suitable for guests or picky family members, since it allows them to add different toppings to get the taste they like. This is why the vegetable stew base itself is kept relatively neutral, allowing for many flavor combinations.

For the stew:
2–3 dried tomatoes
3–4 tomatoes
½ zucchini
½ cucumber
2 scallions
1 tbsp agave syrup
    or 2 medjool dates
6⅔ cups spinach
pinch of cayenne pepper,
    to taste
salt and freshly ground
    black pepper

For the toppings:
4–5 tbsp dried seaweed
handful of Brussels sprouts
    or 2–3 broccoli stems
1 ear of corn
½ bunch cilantro
½ bunch dill
4–5 tbsp pine nuts
tamari, to serve

1 To make the stew, put the dried tomatoes into a small bowl, cover with cold water, and let soak for 30 minutes. Strain the dried tomatoes, saving the soaking water for another recipe. Remove the fresh tomatoes from their stems. Chop the zucchini, cucumber, and scallions, including the greens.

2 To make the six toppings, first put the seaweed into a bowl. Cover it with cold water, and let soak for 30 minutes. Drain just before using. Coarsely chop the Brussels sprouts, or divide the broccoli into small florets. Remove the leaves and silk from the cob of corn. Stand the cob of corn upright on a cutting board. Working from the top downward, use a large, sharp knife to slice the kernels off the cob. Pick the cilantro leaves, and chop the dill coarsely. Without using any oil, toast the pine nuts in a frying pan until they are golden brown. Put each topping into a small bowl.

3 Place all the ingredients for the stew into a blender. Slowly purée the vegetables in the order listed to ensure that the stew has an optimal consistency. Start by puréeing the tomatoes, and then add the zucchini and cucumber but process them only very briefly. Then, add the scallions and the agave syrup or pitted dates. Finally, add the spinach. Season with the cayenne pepper, salt, and pepper.

4 Ladle the vegetable stew into shallow bowls. Set out the toppings on the table in little bowls, and the tamari, to serve, and flavor the stew as desired.

NORI ROLLS

Serves 4, or 8–10 rolls ▪ Preparation time: 30 minutes plus soaking and drying

This is one of my favorite snacks and one that I happily take everywhere with me. Nori rolls are extremely practical, satisfyingly filling, and provide quick protein. They keep in the refrigerator for 2–3 weeks, so I often make a double batch. I like my nori snack hard and crisp, which is why I usually leave the rolls to dry for 8–10 hours. Sometimes, early on in the drying process, I take out a few rolls when the filling is still soft and eat them right away. Later on, I put the rest of the rolls in my snack box.

⅔ cup almonds

1 cup sunflower seeds

½ red onion

½in (1cm) piece fresh ginger

2 dates (medjool are best)

1 tsp garlic powder

1 tsp paprika

2 tbsp cold-pressed almond oil
   or cold-pressed olive oil

4–5 tbsp lemon juice

¼ tsp sea salt

1 tbsp tamari

2 tbsp sesame seeds

½ bunch cilantro

4–5 nori sheets
   (raw or roasted)

You will also need:

sushi-bamboo mats

2 dehydrating trays

food dehydrator

1 Soak the almonds and the sunflower seeds overnight in cold water. Drain just before using. Peel and dice the onion. Peel and finely grate the ginger. Pit the dates.

2 Place the almonds and sunflower seeds into a food processor, and chop them finely. Then add the onion, ginger, dates, garlic, paprika, oil, lemon juice, salt, and tamari. Mix the ingredients until smooth, and then transfer the mixture to a bowl. Without using any oil, toast the sesame seeds in a frying pan. Pick the cilantro leaves, and chop them very finely. Add the cilantro and the sesame seeds to the mixture, using your hand to mix them in.

3 Cut each nori sheet in half. Lay out one sheet horizontally on the bamboo mat. Spread it with a layer of the mixture about ½in (1cm) thick. Leave a free edge along the top about the thickness of your finger. Using your finger and a bit of water, moisten the edge. Roll up the nori sheet like a cigar with the help of the bamboo mat. Repeat with the other sheets of nori until the mixture is used up.

4 Lay out the rolls side by side on the dehydrating trays, leaving a bit of room between them. Dry in a food dehydrator for 5–6 hours at 107.6°F (42°C). Check the degree of dryness occasionally.

TIP If you don't own a dehydrator, you can dry the rolls in the oven. Turn on the oven. Stick a kitchen spoon in the oven door to keep the door slightly ajar. Turn the oven to the lowest setting. The heat should reach about 113°F (45°C). Dry the nori rolls in the oven for about 6 hours. You can also eat the rolls without dehydrating them. Using a sharp knife, cut the rolls into pieces, and eat them right away. However, you will need to chew a bit longer and harder, since nori sheets are a bit tough when they are not dried, although they are still delicious.

Spreads & PASTES

Among my favorite pastes are those inspired by Middle Eastern cuisine, and sesame paste definitely is one of the most useful. In the Middle East, it is known as tahina or tahini and is, like hummus, an essential part of every menu. I have a very personal relationship with hummus due to my Israeli roots. After all, sesame paste is a part of falafel, our national dish. The version made with uncooked peas can hold up on its own. This recipe is from my friend Deborah Felton, whom I got to know through the fantastic and informative Facebook group "Raw Food Wild Riot."

I like to make spreads (see pp.60–61) and sauces (see pp.66–67) in large quantities, since, on the one hand, they freeze well, and, on the other, they can be used as dips or a base for salad dressings. For example, I use date paste in my sandwich on page 64 and as an ingredient in my tomato sauce on page 87. It really pays to have a large amount of date paste in the fridge. Most sauces and spreads have a nut or oil base, which keeps them fresh for 7–10 days, as long as you always use a clean spoon when you remove a portion and keep the sauce containers firmly sealed and refrigerated.

TIP Tahini tastes great as a spread, as a dip for vegetables, or on salads. In my version, I spread tahini on my homemade sandwich bread and sprinkle a few chives and a bit of cayenne pepper over the top.

DATE PASTE

Makes 1 medium jar ▪ Preparation time: 5 minutes

15 dates (medjool are best)
½ lemon

1 If you are using harder dates (medjool is simply the most aromatic and softest kind), soak them in lukewarm water for about 1–2 hours before using them. Then drain the dates, reserving the soaking water.

2 Pit the dates and place them in a blender. Start to purée them on a medium setting for 3 minutes then on the highest setting for 5–7 minutes. Stop the blender occasionally and scrape the mixture down the sides. Here, a dough scraper is very useful. Add the soaking water, if using, 1 tablespoonful at a time, to make the dates easier to purée. But be careful; the date paste must not become too runny! Ideally, you should be able to spoon it out, not pour it out. Juice the lemon, and add a bit of lemon juice to the date paste. Kept well sealed in a jar; it will keep in the refrigerator up to 1 week.

TAHINI

Makes 1 small jar ▪ Preparation time: 20 minutes plus soaking

1⅓ cups sesame seeds
1 garlic clove
½ bunch flat-leaf parsley
½ lemon
1½ tbsp agave syrup
½ tsp coriander seeds
1 tsp sumac or zest of
    ½ organic lemon
salt and freshly ground
    black pepper
crackers or bread, to serve

1 Soak the sesame seeds overnight in cold water. Just before using them, drain the seeds. Peel the garlic. Pick the parsley leaves and chop them. Juice the lemon.

2 Place the soaked sesame seeds and the remaining ingredients—except for the parsley—into a blender. Process on the highest setting for 3–4 minutes. So that the blades can do their work better, you might have to add a bit of water, but never add more than 1 tablespoon at a time. Stop the blender occasionally and, using a spatula or dough scraper, push the paste down the sides.

3 Put the paste into a bowl, add the chopped parsley, and stir. Serve the tahini with crackers or bread.

SUNFLOWER SEED PASTE

Makes 1 small jar ▪ Preparation time: 10 minutes plus soaking

2 cups sunflower seeds

½ bunch chives

½ lemon

½ tsp piri-piri or 1 tsp zahtar

**1 tsp onion powder
(see p.152)**

**¼ tsp salt and freshly ground
black pepper (mixed)**

1 tbsp tamari

crackers or bread, to serve

1 Soak the sunflower seeds overnight in cold water. Drain them just before using them. Chop the chives finely. Juice the lemon.

2 Place all the ingredients, except for the chives, into a blender or food processor. Process on the highest setting for 5 minutes to make a smooth paste. If you like it hot, use the piri-piri instead of zahtar. To make the classic version, use zahtar. Carefully add tablespoonfuls of water to the paste, making sure that the paste does not become too runny.

3 Transfer the paste to a bowl, and stir in the chopped chives. Serve the sunflower seed paste with crackers or bread.

Sprouted pea hummus

Makes 1 small jar ▪ Preparation time: 10 minutes

**12 cups (9oz/250g) pea sprouts
(see p.149)**

1 avocado

2 garlic cloves

1 lemon

½ red onion

**½ cup sesame paste
(see "Tahini" recipe, left)**

¼ cup cold-pressed olive oil

**salt and freshly ground
black pepper**

1 Rinse the sprouts. Slice the avocado lengthwise in half, remove the pit, and scoop out the avocado flesh. Peel the garlic, and cut it into large pieces. Juice the lemon.

2 Place all the ingredients into a food processor. Process on the highest setting for 5 minutes until everything is finely chopped and the mixture is thick and creamy.

MISO & CASHEW cream SOUP

Serves 2–3 ▪ Preparation time: 10 minutes plus soaking

This is, without doubt, a filling soup for cold days and is good for you, too. This recipe comes from my friend Irina. When I asked her what her favorite raw food recipe was, she prepared this soup on the spot—of course, we were sitting in the kitchen! Since then, it has been part of my standard repertoire, and I hope it will soon be part of yours.

1⅓ cups cashews

**1 tbsp dried seaweed
(wakame, nori, or arame)**

½ lime

1½ tbsp dark miso paste

pinch of cayenne pepper

**½ tsp cold-pressed
sesame oil**

1 Soak the cashews overnight in cold water. Just before using them, drain the cashews. After a brief rinse, soak the seaweed in cold water (arame or nori for about 5 minutes, the wakame for about 10 minutes). Drain the seaweed just before using it. Juice the lime.

2 Place all the ingredients, except for the seaweed, into a blender. Add 2 cups water, and purée until the mixture is thick and creamy. Transfer the mixture to a pan, and warm it gently over low heat until it reaches about 104°F (40°C). Add the seaweed, and stir. Serve warm.

TIP Those who do not follow strict raw food guidelines can substitute toasted sesame oil for cold-pressed sesame oil. This lends the dish an intense nutty taste.

✳ *Sandwich* BREAD

Makes 10–12 sandwiches ▪ Preparation time: 1½ hours plus soaking and drying

Used to make sandwiches with a variety of sauces and several layers, this bread truly is very special. It is a good idea to make a large quantity of everything, because you can freeze it and defrost it at least once. With this recipe, and a bit of practice and patience, you will be able to make wonderful "genuine" bread—enough to last you several weeks.

2¾ cups dried tomatoes

1 cup ground flaxseed

3½ cups sunflower seeds

1 apple

6½ cups chopped zucchini

4–5 tbsp lemon juice

¾ cup cold-pressed olive oil

¼ cup date paste (see p.60)

1 tsp sea salt

7 tbsp dried Herbes de Provence

You will also need:

4 dehydrating trays

food dehydrator

1 Soak the dried tomatoes overnight in cold water. Shortly before using, drain the tomatoes. Working separately in batches, place the flaxseed and the sunflower seeds into a food processor, and grind them into flour. Cut the apple into quarters and core it.

2 Place all the ingredients, except for the ground flaxseed, sunflower seeds, and herbs, into a blender. Purée until creamy. Transfer the mixture to a large bowl. Add the ground sunflower seeds and the herbs. Using a whisk, combine everything thoroughly. Then, add the ground flaxseed, and whisk everything again vigorously. Make sure that no clumps form.

3 Using an offset spatula, spread the mixture over the entire surface of the dehydrating trays, about ½in (1cm) thick. Place the trays in the food dehydrator, and dry them at 104°F (40°C). After 4 hours, check to see whether the mixture can be sliced. When it is dry enough to slice, cut each layer into 9 squares, and then dry for another 2–3 hours. When the surface of the bread is dry enough, carefully turn over each slice, and continue drying until they reach the desired degree of dehydration. This takes 3–4 hours.

TIP The sandwich shown on the right is a creation of the Munich raw food restaurant Gratitude—Organic Eatery. To make it, you will need 2 slices of sandwich bread. Spread one slice with 1 tablespoon of mustard sauce (see p.66) and the other with 1 tablespoon of tomato sauce (see p.67). On top of one of the pieces of bread, place a thick layer of sprouts (mung beans, wasabi sprouts, or a mixture of sprouts), 3 slices of tomatoes, 2 slices of cucumber, salad greens, and arugula to taste, a few pieces of dehydrated red pepper, and a thin layer of dehydrated shallots. Top it all off with a thin layer of sunflower seed paste (see p.61), and then cover with the second piece of bread. For a sandwich that not only tastes delicious but also looks delicious, cut the sandwich on the diagonal with a serrated knife.

* MUSTARD SAUCE

Makes 1 large jar ▪ Preparation time: 15 minutes plus soaking

1 cup mustard seeds

2¼ cups almonds

3 tbsp lemon juice

pinch of sea salt

1 tbsp date paste (see p.60)

1 Soak the mustard seeds overnight in cold water. Drain them just before using.

2 Place all the ingredients into a blender or food processor. Add ¾ cup of water. Process on the highest setting for 5 minutes.

Sunflower seed sauce

Makes 1 large jar ▪ Preparation time: 20 minutes plus soaking

1 Soak the tomatoes and the sunflower seeds overnight in cold water. Drain them just before using.

2 Place all the ingredients into a blender or food processor. Purée on the highest setting for 5 minutes.

1⅓ cups dried tomatoes
2 cups sunflower seeds
4 tbsp cold-pressed olive oil
1 tsp dried Herbes de Provence
½ tsp paprika
¼ tsp cayenne pepper
salt and ground black pepper

TOMATO SAUCE

Makes 16fl oz (500ml) ▪ Preparation time: 20 minutes plus soaking

1 Soak the dried tomatoes overnight in cold water. Drain them just before using. Remove the stems from the fresh tomatoes and cut them in half or quarters. Remove the stem from the red pepper, seed it, and cut out the pith. Peel the garlic, and pit the dates.

2 Place all the ingredients, except for the herbs and seasoning, into a blender or food processor. Purée on the highest setting for 5 minutes. Pick the herb leaves, chop them finely, and stir them into the sauce. Season with sea salt and pepper.

2⅔ cups dried tomatoes
1lb (450g) tomatoes
1 red pepper
2 garlic cloves
4 dates
4 tbsp cold-pressed olive oil
2 tbsp apple vinegar
4 sprigs flat-leaf parsley
  or basil
sea salt and ground black pepper

Garlic sauce

Makes 1 large jar ▪ Preparation time: 15 minutes plus soaking

1 Soak the cashews overnight in cold water. Drain them just before using. Peel the garlic and put it through a garlic press.

2 Place all the ingredients, except for the cucumber, into a blender. Purée on the highest setting for 5 minutes. If needed, you can add a bit of water to make the mixture creamier.

3 Slice the cucumber lengthwise in half. Using a spoon, scrape out the seeds. Grate the cucumber finely, and stir it into the sauce.

2 cups cashews
2 garlic cloves
¼ cup lemon juice
¼ tsp sea salt
½–1 cucumber (depending on the consistency desired)

ARUGULA & PEAR salad

Serves 4 ▪ Preparation time: 15 minutes

For the salad:

2 pears

1 bunch arugula

1 large handful of baby spinach

2 tbsp chopped walnuts

dried vegetables, to serve

For the dressing:

4 tbsp apple cider vinegar

2 tbsp cold-pressed sesame oil
(see tip, p.63)

1 tsp agave syrup

pinch of dried rosemary

salt and freshly ground
black pepper

1 To make the salad, cut the pears into quarters, remove the cores, and thinly slice them into half-moon-shaped pieces. Put the pears into a bowl. Add the arugula, spinach, and walnuts, and toss gently.

2 To make the dressing, whisk together all the ingredients. Season with salt and pepper. Pour the dressing over the salad and toss gently to combine.

3 Divide the salad between four plates. Sprinkle the dried vegetables over the salads before serving.

Those who like a rustic feel to their food can use ume vinegar and ginger, a dash of olive oil, balsamic vinegar, salt, and pepper instead of tamari. You also can use freshly grated horseradish instead of ginger.

Japanese CUCUMBER SALAD

Serves 3 ▪ Preparation time: 15 minutes plus marinating

1 Slice the wakame into small pieces. Put them into a bowl, add cold water, and soak for 10 minutes. If you are using arame, which comes shredded, it needs only a brief soak. Slice the nori into short, thin, strips. Peel the kohlrabi. Slice the kohlrabi and cucumber into bite-size pieces.

2 To make the dressing, peel the ginger and grate it finely. Add the ginger to the remaining ingredients, except for the sesame seeds. Add 2 tablespoons water, and stir well.

3 Drain the seaweed and place it in a bowl. Stir in the cucumber and kohlrabi. Pour the dressing over the salad. Mix everything together, using your hands for the best result.

4 Put the salad into the refrigerator to marinate for 15 minutes. Stir in the sesame seeds just before serving.

1¾oz (50g) dried wakame or
  arame seaweed

2 nori seaweed sheets, raw

1 kohlrabi

1 cucumber

1 (½in/1cm) piece of ginger

dash of tamari

2 tbsp ume vinegar

1–2 pinches of wasabi powder,
  to taste

pinch of cayenne pepper

squeeze of lemon juice

1 tbsp white sesame seeds

1 tbsp black sesame seeds

TIP The dressing tastes even better when you stir in the mashed flesh of ½ avocado. The lemon juice ensures that the avocado retains its lovely green color.

TOMATO AND SEAWEED salad

Makes 1 large portion ▪ Preparation time: 10 minutes plus soaking

Tomatoes and seaweed complement each other well. This is a light, fresh salad that I enjoy with crackers and a spread.

1 Soak the seaweed in cold water for at least 10 minutes. Drain the seaweed just before using it. Remove the stems from the tomatoes, and cut them into bite-size pieces. Peel the onion and slice it finely.

2 In a bowl, whisk together the two types of oil with the tamari and ume vinegar. Add the seaweed, tomato, onion, and sesame seeds, and toss everything gently to combine.

¼oz (10g) wakame and arame
  seaweed (mixed)

2 medium tomatoes

½ red onion

2 tbsp cold-pressed sesame oil

1 tbsp neutral vegetable oil

3 tbsp tamari

1 tbsp ume vinegar

1 tsp sesame seeds

*Cabbage &
*AVOCADO SLAW

Serves 1–2 ▪ Preparation time: 20 minutes plus marinating

This combination might sound strange at first, but you will discover how well the individual ingredients go together. If you do serve this very filling salad to guests, skeptical glances will turn into approving nods after the first bite. Try it! And save the cabbage juice. Thin it with a bit of water, and enjoy it as a drink. It is very good for digestion.

¼ **head green cabbage**

1 tbsp sea salt

2 avocados

1 tsp lemon juice

salt and freshly ground
  black pepper

pinch of cayenne pepper
  (optional)

1 orange

3 tbsp pomegranate seeds

1 Cut out the core from the cabbage. Grate it very finely using a grater or a food processor. Combine the cabbage and sea salt, knead thoroughly for 2–3 minutes, and let it marinate for at least 15 minutes.

2 Put the cabbage into a colander set over a bowl, and press out the juice. Let drain. Save the salty cabbage juices that have been released to drink later, if you choose. Slice the avocados lengthwise in half, peel them, and remove the pits. Using a fork, mash 1½ avocados in a bowl. Add 1 teaspoon of lemon juice and the cabbage. Mix well to

combine. Season with a bit of pepper and, if needed, salt. Be careful since the cabbage will be a bit salty. Add the cayenne pepper if you want to give the salad a bit of heat.

3 Peel the orange, being careful to remove all the white pith. Cut out the orange segments. Dice the remaining avocado into bite-size cubes. Add the avocado and orange to the cabbage, and toss.

4 To serve, place the salad on one or two plates, and sprinkle the pomegranate seeds over the top.

TIP There is a great trick for seeding pomegranates. Unfortunately, I just learned about it only after years of having my clothes splattered with their juice. Fill a large bowl with water. Make a cut in the pomegranate. Open up the cut under water. The seeds will plop into the water, and no juice will splatter!

SPICY MANGO SALAD

Serves 1–2 ▪ Preparation time: 15 minutes

As is the case in many recipes, it is also true here that if you want to follow a strict raw food diet, don't toast the pine nuts. I admit that, occasionally, I gladly forfeit a few raw food "points" for the taste of toasted seeds sprinkled on my salad!

For the salad:

1 mango

1 kohlrabi

2 large handfuls baby spinach

½–1 fresh red chili pepper

½ bunch cilantro

½ cup dried cranberries

½ cob of corn, shucked

¼ cup pine nuts

For the dressing:

2 tbsp cold-pressed olive oil

1 tbsp lime juice

1 tsp orange juice

salt

1 tsp agave syrup

1 To make the salad, peel the mango. Cut the flesh from the pit, and then chop it into bite-size pieces. Peel the kohlrabi and slice it into cubes, making sure they are not too small. Cut the stem end off the chili pepper, seed it, and finely chop the chili. (Be sure to wash your hands immediately afterward and avoid contact with your eyes.) Pick the cilantro leaves. Quarter the cranberries, or chop them coarsely, depending on their size. Stand the cob of corn upright on a cutting board. Working from the top downward, use a large, sharp knife to slice the kernels off the cob.

2 Carefully combine all the ingredients for the dressing in a bowl. Add all the salad ingredients and toss gently. Add the raw pine nuts or, to increase the flavor, pine nuts that you have toasted in a frying pan without using any oil.

TIP Adjust the amount of chili pepper you use according to how hot the chili is. I don't use very hot chilies, since the salad can become unpalatable very quickly. While it is true you can better gauge the heat by using chili powder, the fresh chili added to this salad makes it more delicious when used judiciously. If you usually shy away from using fresh chili peppers, be brave, and give it a try. It isn't all that hard!

FENNEL & CILANTRO *salad*

Serves 1–2 ▪ Preparation time: 20 minutes

Whenever I find fresh fennel, I always buy a few bulbs and prepare this quick, uncomplicated salad. It is very easy to put together and tastes superb!

For the salad:

2 medium fennel bulbs, with
  fronds

1 large tomato, or 2 small ones

bunch of cilantro

3 tbsp sesame seeds

For the dressing:

1 tsp agave syrup

squeeze of lemon juice

1 tbsp balsamic vinegar

1 tbsp cold-pressed sesame oil

salt and freshly ground
  black pepper

1 Cut out the core of the fennel bulbs. Using a mandolin or a sharp knife, finely slice the bulbs. Reserve the fronds. Remove the tomato stem. Cut the tomato into pieces, making sure the pieces are not too small. Pick the cilantro leaves and chop them coarsely. Chop the fennel fronds coarsely.

2 Place the agave syrup, lemon juice, vinegar, oil, salt, and pepper into a bowl. Whisk well to combine. Add the fennel, tomatoes, cilantro, and sesame seeds. Toss the salad, and let it steep for 15–20 minutes before serving.

TIP You can serve the salad warm if you have a food dehydrator. Put the salad, in its serving bowl, in the dehydrator for 1 hour. Although it does not conform to strict raw food guidelines, toasting the sesame seeds releases their nutty flavor. When I make this recipe, I happily turn a blind eye and use toasted sesame seeds.

SUSHI MEDLEY

Makes 3 maki rolls or 18 pieces ▪ Preparation time: 30 minutes

Before my raw food period began, I never realized that there was raw food sushi. How could there be? At the very least, sushi rice has to be cooked. I did not think there was an alternative to rice that equaled it in flavor. In New York, I finally made the acquaintance of this sensational version. When you first start making sushi, it is easiest to slice the sushi rolls into large pieces so that you avoid a lot of cutting, since it is when you are slicing sushi rolls, especially when you are a beginner, that mess occurs.

For the rice substitute:

1 kohlrabi

4 parsnips

1 tbsp tamari

1 tbsp ume vinegar
   or apple cider vinegar

1 tsp cold-pressed sesame oil

3 nori sheets, raw

For the filling
   (your pick of vegetables):

1 avocado

1 carrot

½ cucumber

4 radishes

1 handful of snow pea pods

3 scallions

2 tbsp takuan
   (pickled daikon radish)

1 tsp wasabi or grated
   horseradish

3 tbsp white sesame seeds

You will also need:

sushi bamboo mat

1 Peel the kohlrabi. Place it into a food processor, and blend it until it is the size of grains of rice. Transfer the kohlrabi to a bowl. Repeat this step with the parsnips. Add the parsnips to the kohlrabi, add the liquid ingredients, and stir.

2 To make the filling, first prepare the vegetables you have chosen (for example, remove the avocado pit, or seed the cucumber) and slice them into thin strips about ¼in (½cm) in diameter.

3 Place a nori sheet on the bamboo mat. Cover it with a layer of the ricelike mixture about ¼in (½cm) thick. Leave an edge free along the top the thickness of a finger. Press down firmly on the chopped mixture using the palm of your hand.

4 Spread a horizontal line of wasabi or grated horseradish along the center of the "rice." Place several pieces of vegetables of your choice on top, and sprinkle them with a few sesame seeds. Moisten the free edge with a bit of water. Using the bamboo mat, roll up the nori sheet from bottom to top, pressing down lightly as you do so. Repeat with the other sheets of nori. Don't give up if the first rolls are a bit lopsided and bent—it takes a bit of patience. With practice, your rolls will turn out beautifully.

5 Using a sharp knife, slice the rolls into pieces as thick as you like. For authentic sushi size, cut the roll in the middle, and then divide each half into thirds. This gives six pieces per roll.

TIP Instead of wasabi or horseradish, you can also use leftover sauces or pastes as flavorings. My friend Buffi's favorite version is mango with oregano and cashew cheese (see p.26). The combination never would have occurred to me, but this example just goes to show how varied tastes can be!

*CAESAR *salad*

Serves 1–2 ▪ Preparation time: 20 minutes

A typical American Caesar salad has always been one of my favorites. I would go far for that salad dressing! I was really happy when I found a way of transforming the classic recipe into a raw version in only a few steps—just remember to leave out the croutons!

For the salad:

1 head romaine lettuce
　or 3 romaine hearts

1 tomato

½ red onion

For the dressing:

1 small garlic clove

1 celery stick

2 tbsp cold-pressed olive oil

1 tbsp pumpkin seeds

2 tsp lemon juice

1 tsp tamari

1 tsp white-miso paste

1 tsp balsamic vinegar

1 Tear the lettuce leaves into large pieces. Remove the tomato stem, and cut the tomato into eight pieces. Peel the onion and slice it into thin strips.

2 To make the dressing, peel the garlic. Cut the celery into pieces. Place all the ingredients for the dressing into a blender. Purée on the highest setting for 2–3 minutes to a make a creamy dressing.

3 Put the romaine lettuce, tomato, and onion in a large bowl, add the salad dressing, and toss well to combine. Serve in small bowls or plates.

PASTA

When I started eating raw food, my biggest concern was that I would no longer be able to eat pasta noodles! And when I first saw raw zucchini noodles, I didn't feel all that much better. Dispirited, I thought, "Those vegetable spirals can never, ever, replace my pasta!" But then I tried them, and now I don't feel like anything is lacking when I eat a lovely zucchini or cucumber pasta with truffle pesto. I hope you will have exactly the same experience!

In my opinion, one of the greatest raw food tools is the spiralizer (see p.154), something that a really smart person invented! Harder vegetables, such as carrots, kohlrabi, or red beets are more difficult to spiralize and require a bit of practice. My friend Irina is an absolute virtuoso at spiralizing. She's an exceptionally gifted raw food cook, and, every time I see her, she turns something into spirals for me. Still, I continue to cut certain types of harder vegetables, such as kohlrabi, into small cubes, not spirals. If you succeed in spiralizing such vegetables, even better!

TIP The easiest way to catch the spirals is to hold the salad bowl at an angle under the spiralizer so that the noodles land right in the bowl. Another good thing about the spiralizer is that it spiralizes only the firm cucumber flesh and spits out the seeds, ensuring the cucumber noodles are nice and firm.

* CUCUMBER & AVOCADO PASTA

Serves 2 ▪ Preparation time: 20 minutes

This is one of my favorite recipes, since it combines all the best raw food qualities in a dish that I cherish. It is quick to make, light, and refreshing. Normally, raw food has to fight against the general prejudice that it isn't filling enough. This wonderful meal proves the opposite! The cucumber is nicely filling, and the avocado provides a healthy source of fat—simply perfect.

For the pasta:

1 kohlrabi

1 fresh ear of corn

2 scallions

1½–2 cucumbers

3–4 cherry tomatoes

1 tbsp black sesame seeds

pinch of ground chipotle powder
   or cayenne pepper

6–8 leaves Thai basil (optional)

For the dressing:

1 avocado

4 tbsp tamari

2 tbsp ume vinegar

You will also need:

spiralizer

1 Peel and dice the kohlrabi, or cut it into spirals using a spiralizer. Shuck the corn, removing the silk. Stand the cob of corn upright on a cutting board, and, working from the top downward, use a large, sharp knife to slice the kernels off the cob. Finely slice the scallions, including the greens. Use the spiralizer to turn the unpeeled cucumber into cucumber noodles. Mix the vegetables together in a large bowl. Slice the cherry tomatoes.

2 To make the dressing, slice the avocado lengthwise in half, remove the pit, and scoop out the avocado flesh. Put the avocado flesh in a bowl, mash the avocado with a fork, and stir in the tamari and ume vinegar. Gently stir the vegetables and the dressing together, to combine.

3 Divide the pasta between 2 plates. Sprinkle sesame seeds and cherry tomatoes over the top, and sprinkle with chipotle powder or cayenne pepper. Serve immediately so that the cucumber does not become too watery. For an intense flavor, add Thai basil, which works very well in this dish.

TIP Add the dressing to the cucumbers just before serving if you want to prepare this dish more than 30 minutes in advance. You will not need any additional salt, since both the ume vinegar and the tamari are salty enough. Due to its high water content, cucumber is highly beneficial for the body. It is good for your skin, helps your body to detox, and balances the pH in the body. These are great side effects, but the main reason this dish has ended up in this book is because it is simply irresistible!

PASTA SAUCES

These three sauces are among my absolute favorites. Having a few good sauces in the fridge always comes in very handy, and this is especially true in raw food cuisine. Each of these recipes is very different, goes with practically anything, and is very versatile.

Mushroom sauce

Serves 1–2 ▪ Preparation time: 10 minutes

3 cups brown mushrooms
2 tbsp flat-leaf parsley
2–3 squeezes lemon juice
3 tbsp cold-pressed olive oil
½ tsp sea salt
1 tbsp pine nuts

Rub the mushrooms with a paper towel. Finely chop the parsley. Place all the ingredients into a blender or a food processor. For a chunky sauce, purée for 2–3 minutes on a low setting. For a creamy sauce, purée for 3–4 minutes on the highest setting.

Serves 1–2 ▪ Preparation time: 5 minutes

Truffle and sesame sauce

3 tbsp sesame paste   **1 tsp honey or agave syrup**
1 tsp truffle oil   **pinch of sea salt**
1 tbsp white wine vinegar

Place all the ingredients into a bowl. Whisk well until the sauce has emulsified, or mix briefly with an electric mixer.

Tomato sauce

Serves 1–2 ▪ Preparation time: 10 minutes

6 dried tomatoes   **salt and freshly ground**
3 beefsteak tomatoes   **black pepper**
½ red onion   **pinch of paprika**
1 tbsp date paste (see p.60)
1 tbsp tamari

Soak the dried tomatoes in cold water for 1 hour, and then drain just before using. Reserve the water. Remove the stems from the fresh tomatoes, and cut the tomatoes into quarters. Peel and coarsely dice the onion. Place all the ingredients into a food processor or blender. For a chunky sauce, purée for 2–3 minutes on a low setting. For a creamy sauce, purée on the highest setting for 3–4 minutes. If the sauce is too thick, add a bit of the tomato soaking water.

GLASS NOODLES *with* ARUGULA & *sunflower-seed pesto*

Serves 1–2 ▪ Preparation time: 20 minutes plus soaking

This pesto tastes really delicious with all kinds of noodles, such as kelp noodles, glass noodles, or vegetable noodles! I like it best on glass noodles. They are softened in hot water for a few minutes and so are not really raw, but I waive the rules a bit here. Those whose goal is to eat 100 percent raw would be better off sticking to kelp noodles, the raw alternative to glass noodles. I like both, but, for this pesto, I prefer to use "regular" glass noodles.

For the pesto:

**4 heaping tbsp
   sunflower seeds**

1 garlic clove

½ lemon

handful of arugula

3 tbsp cold-pressed olive oil

½ tsp salt

You will also need:

2 nests glass noodles

1 Soak the sunflower seeds overnight in cold water. Put a sieve over a bowl. Just before using, drain the sunflower seeds. Retain the soaking liquid. Peel the garlic. Juice the lemon.

2 Place the sunflower seeds, the remaining pesto ingredients, and 4 tablespoons of the soaking water into a blender. Purée on the lowest setting for 1–2 minutes.

3 Put 2 cups water in a pan, bring it to a boil, and boil briefly. Remove the pan from the stove. When the water has stopped boiling, add the glass noodles, cover the pan, and leave the noodles to steep for 7–10 minutes. When the noodles have softened but still have a bite (they will continue to cook a bit), drain the noodles in a colander. Transfer them to a large bowl.

4 Pour the pesto over the noodles, toss well to combine, and serve.

TIP

Pesto and garlic are thought to go together hand in hand. I dislike having the smell of garlic waft about me for the rest of the day, so I make my pesto without garlic—and it tastes delicious!

Spinach pesto

Serves 2–3 ▪ Preparation time: 10 minutes plus soaking

Soak the almonds overnight in cold water. Drain just before using them. Juice the lemon. Place all the ingredients into a blender or food processor. Purée on a low setting for 1–2 minutes.

3 tbsp almonds
½ lemon
3⅓ cups baby spinach
1 tsp apple cider vinegar
½ cup cold-pressed olive oil
pinch of cayenne pepper
½ tsp sea salt

TRUFFLE PESTO

Serves 2–3 ▪ Preparation time: 10 minutes plus soaking

Soak the cashews overnight in cold water. Drain just before using them. Juice the lemon. Place all the ingredients into a blender or food processor. Purée on the lowest setting for 1–2 minutes. It is best when the pesto is still a bit chunky.

¾ cup cashews
½ lemon
3 tbsp neutral vegetable oil
1 tsp truffle oil
salt

Red pepper pesto

Serves 2–3 ▪ Preparation time: 10 minutes plus soaking

Soak the cashews overnight in cold water. Drain just before using them. Remove the stems from the peppers, seed them, and cut out the pith. Pick the cilantro leaves. Place all the ingredients into a blender or a food processor, and purée on the lowest setting for 1–2 minutes. The pesto is best when it is still a bit chunky.

3 tbsp cashews
½ red bell pepper
½ yellow bell pepper
¼ bunch cilantro
½ cup cold-pressed olive oil
2–3 squeezes lemon juice
salt and freshly ground
    black pepper

BASIL PESTO

Serves 2–3 ▪ Preparation time: 10 minutes plus soaking

Soak the cashews overnight in cold water. Drain just before using them. Grate the lemon zest, and then juice the lemon. Place all the ingredients in a blender or food processor. Purée on the lowest setting for 1–2 minutes. The basil pesto is best when it is still a bit chunky.

3 tbsp cashews
½ organic lemon
1 bunch basil
2 garlic cloves
3 tbsp cold-pressed olive oil
3 tbsp pine nuts
salt

MEDITERRANEAN GLASS NOODLES

Serves 2 ▪ Preparation time: 20 minutes

Since glass noodles (see p.88) are used in this recipe, it is not 100 percent raw. But glass noodles are a perfect match for vegetables, pestos, sauces, and dressings. They are easily prepared and versatile, and you can quickly create a huge variety of dishes with them. I freely admit that I adore them!

For the noodles:

2 nests of glass noodles

2 carrots

½ cucumber

¾ cup cherry tomatoes

2⅓ cups brown mushrooms

2 scallions

4 medium romaine lettuce leaves

½ bunch cilantro

1 tbsp sesame seeds

1 tbsp sunflower seeds

1 tbsp pine nuts

For the sauce:

1 celery stick

5 cherry tomatoes

1 zucchini

celery salt (see p.150)
  or sea salt

2–3 tbsp dried tomatoes soaking
  water, or water

1 To prepare the glass noodles, briefly boil 2 cups water in a pan, and remove the pan from the stove. When the water has stopped boiling, add the glass noodles and let them steep for 7–10 minutes. Drain the noodles when soft but not too soft. (They will continue cooking a bit.)

2 Peel the carrots. Thinly slice or dice the unpeeled cucumber, the tomatoes, and the mushrooms, and place them in a large bowl. Finely slice the scallions and the lettuce leaves into long, thin strips and add them to the bowl. Add the drained noodles to the bowl, and toss.

3 To make the sauce, place all the ingredients in a blender. Purée on a low setting so that the sauce will still be a bit chunky. If the sauce is too thick, thin it with a bit of dried tomato soaking water, or water. Pick the cilantro leaves and place them in a small bowl. Add the sesame seeds, sunflower seeds, and pine nuts, and stir.

4 Pour the sauce over the noodles and vegetables, and toss well to combine. Sprinkle the chopped cilantro, sesame and sunflower seeds, and pine nuts on top, and serve.

TIP You can, of course, make a smooth sauce, too. Put all the ingredients for the sauce in a blender, and purée on the highest setting for 2–3 minutes until nice and creamy. Personally, I prefer the chunkier version for this dish.

* MEDITERRANEAN RATATOUILLE

Serves 3–4 ▪ Preparation time: 30 minutes

For the vegetables:

1 lemon

1 medium eggplant

salt

2 red sweet banana peppers
   or red peppers

½ yellow bell pepper

½ green bell pepper

1 beefsteak tomato

½ zucchini

¼ white onion

½ bunch flat-leaf parsley

2 sprigs thyme, plus a few
   extra, to decorate

2 sprigs marjoram or
   1 tsp dried marjoram

For the sauce:

½ red pepper

2 beefsteak tomatoes

½ cucumber

1 garlic clove

2 tbsp cold-pressed olive oil

1 tbsp balsamic vinegar

1 tbsp apple cider vinegar

1 tsp agave syrup

salt and freshly ground
   black pepper

1 Juice the lemon. Cut the eggplant into bite-size pieces, place it in a bowl, and add 1 teaspoon salt and the lemon juice. Stir to combine. Cover the bowl and let marinate for 30 minutes.

2 In the meantime, prepare the peppers by cutting out the stems, seeding, and removing the pith. Cut out the tomato stem. Slice the peppers, tomato, and zucchini into bite-size pieces. Peel and dice the onion. Pick the herb leaves and chop them.

3 Put all the ingredients for the vegetables into a large bowl, toss well to combine, and let them marinate briefly. In the meantime, to make the sauce, finely dice the red pepper and the tomatoes. Cut the unpeeled cucumber into pieces. Peel the garlic. Place the vegetables and the remaining sauce ingredients into a blender or food processor. Purée for 1–2 minutes on the highest setting.

4 Toss the sauce and the sliced vegetables, and season with salt and pepper. Divide the ratatouille between the plates, and garnish with sprigs of thyme. Mushroom rice (see p.115) goes very well with the ratatouille as a side dish.

TIP Warming the ratatouille in a food dehydrator at 104°F (40°C) is a great option. It takes 1–2 hours and turns this into a lovely winter dish. You can also warm the dish in the oven for 2–3 hours. Turn the oven on low, and place a kitchen spoon in the oven door to keep it slightly ajar. This will maintain the desired temperature.

My favorite Vietnamese dish is Nem Cuon—fresh Vietnamese spring rolls. They are, like glass noodles, not strictly raw, but the filling makes up for it. For a lively dinner party, set out the prepared fillings on the table, and let the guests make the rolls themselves— it's very communal!

SPRING ROLLS
with ginger dip

Makes 4–5 rolls ▪ Preparation time: 30–40 minutes

1 Peel the carrots. Using a thin peeler, shave the carrots into slices then cut into thin strips. Cut the zucchini and cucumber in half lengthwise, and scrape out the seeds with a spoon. Cut both into thin strips. Cut the tomatoes in half, remove the stems and seeds, and dice.

2 Cut the celery and the scallions, including the greens, into long, thin strips no longer than the width of the rice paper wrappers or cabbage leaves. Slice the avocado lengthwise in half and remove the pit. Peel the avocado, and slice each half lengthwise into eighths. If you want (but then know that the recipe will no longer be 100 percent raw), lightly toast the sesame seeds in a frying pan without using any oil. Soak the noodles in water for 5–10 minutes. (If using kelp noodles, soak in cold water; if using glass noodles, soak in warm water.) Cut the iceberg lettuce into thin strips.

3 To make the dip, grate the ginger finely, place it in a small serving bowl, and whisk in the tamari or soy sauce and ume vinegar.

4 Fill a wide shallow bowl with water. Put the rice paper wrappers very briefly in the water then place them on a cutting board. Immediately spread the vegetables of your choice on each wrapper, and sprinkle sesame seeds over the top, leaving the edges free. Fold the two sides of each wrapper over the filling, and roll up the wrapper from the bottom. Just before you finish rolling, moisten your finger again, run it over all the edges, then "glue" your wrap shut.

5 Sprinkle the sesame seeds over the spring rolls. Serve the ginger dip on the side.

For the filling:
3 carrots

2 small zucchini

½ cucumber

2–3 tomatoes

2 celery sticks

1 bunch scallions

1 avocado

3–4 tbsp sesame seeds

9oz (250g) kelp noodles or glass noodles

½ head iceberg lettuce

For the dip:
1 (¾in/2cm) piece of fresh ginger

2¾ tbsp tamari or soy sauce

1 tbsp ume vinegar

You will also need:
5 rice paper wrappers, or marinated cabbage leaves (see tip)

TIP Instead of rice paper wrappers, you can use cabbage leaves to make a genuinely raw version. Add 1 teaspoon lemon juice to 2 cups of water. Add a few drops of sesame oil and a pinch of salt. Place 4–5 cabbage leaves in the water, and soak for 15–20 minutes. This will make the leaves pliable. Fill and roll up the leaves using the same method as for the wrappers in step 4. They are very delicious.

RAVIOLI

Serves 2 ▪ Preparation time: 40 minutes plus soaking

As a rule, my recipes are not too difficult and can be described as lying somewhere between dead easy and foolproof. Making this dish, however, calls for a bit of finesse. It is a delicate dish, suitable for a romantic dinner or other festive occasion.

For the ravioli:

⅔ **cup cashews**

1 **medium zucchini**

1 **small daikon radish**

½ **tsp salt**

handful of basil leaves

4 **sprigs flat-leaf parsley**

8–10 **mint leaves**

1 **tsp onion powder**
   (see p.152)

½ **tsp sea salt**

1½ **tbsp cold-pressed olive oil**

You will also need:

⅓ **cup cashews, to serve**

pinch of sea salt

2 **small red radishes**

1 Soak the cashews overnight in cold water. Drain them just before using.

2 Peel the zucchini and radish as thinly as possible. Cut off the long radish tail. Cut the vegetables lengthwise into very fine slices. This will be easiest if you use a mandolin or vegetable slicer. Put the slices in lukewarm salted water for 1–2 hours.

3 In the meantime, place the cashews and the remaining ingredients for the filling into a blender or a food processor, and purée until the mixture has a creamy but still firm consistency. If needed, carefully add a bit of water a tablespoonful at a time.

4 Lay out the slices of zucchini and radish on the work surface. Place a small dollop of the filling on the lower half of a slice, and then fold over the top half. Lightly press along the outside edges of the folded slices with your fingers. The purée will hold the vegetable slices together.

5 Finely grate the cashews or chop them in a mini food processor. They will stand in for Parmesan cheese. Season with the sea salt, and stir to combine. Cut up the red radishes to serve on the side.

6 Divide the ravioli between two plates, sprinkle the grated cashews on top, and serve. Tomato sauce (see p.87) goes very well with the ravioli.

TIP Soaking the zucchini and daikon radish in salted water makes them pliable and easy to work with. The daikon radish lends the dish a fresh, crisp note. If you don't like its taste, just use the zucchini.

* Asian KELP NOODLES

Serves 2 ▪ Preparation time: 20 minutes plus soaking

This is one of my favorite recipes, one that I make often. For all pasta-lovers, kelp noodles are an absolutely fantastic basic ingredient. They can be transformed into countless different dishes. And each time I eat them, they taste a little different. Here is my absolute favorite version.

For the noodles:

12oz (340g) kelp noodles
handful of peas
   (fresh or frozen)
½ cucumber
½ red pepper
1 carrot
1 small red onion
3 scallions
1 tbsp black sesame seeds

For the sauce:

1 ripe avocado
3 tbsp tamari
½–1 tbsp ume vinegar
1 tsp cold-pressed sesame oil
pinch of cayenne pepper
pinch of salt

1 Soak the noodles in cold water for at least 5–10 minutes to make it easier to separate them. Drain the noodles. Defrost the peas, if frozen.

2 In the meantime, cut the unpeeled cucumber lengthwise in half. Scrape out the seeds with a spoon so that the cucumber stays nice and crisp. Dice the cucumber. Remove the stem from the red pepper, seed it, cut out the pith, and dice. Peel the carrot. Using a thin peeler, shave the carrot into strips. Peel and finely slice the red onion. Finely slice the scallions, including the greens. Put the kelp noodles into a large bowl, add the vegetables, and toss gently to combine.

3 To make the sauce, slice the avocado lengthwise in half, remove the pit, and scoop out the avocado flesh. Put the flesh into a small bowl and mash it with a fork. Add 1–2 teaspoons water, and stir everything together until smooth. Season with the tamari, ume vinegar (be careful; it has a strong taste), sesame oil, cayenne pepper, and salt. Stir everything thoroughly to combine.

4 Pour the sauce over the noodles, and toss. Divide the noodles between the plates or bowls. Sprinkle some sesame seeds over the top, and serve.

TIP Sometimes I prepare this dish just for myself, ensuring leftovers, and effectively making tomorrow's lunch. Usually this Asian noodle dish tastes even better the next day, since the noodles have marinated in the sauce overnight. But don't be alarmed if the dish has turned a bit brown. This is caused by the avocado, which oxidizes quickly. The smoky flavor of the chipotle powder goes very well with this dish.

ASIAN-STYLE VEGETABLES
with cauliflower rice

Serves 4 ▪ Preparation time: 45 minutes plus marinating

This dish is so delicious that all the chopping really pays off. I like to leave the vegetables in the marinade a bit longer so they are well steeped and the dish seems more typically Asian. With a shorter marinating time, the vegetables stay crisper.

For the vegetables:

1 red pepper

2 carrots

handful of snow pea pods

1 small red onion

2–3 broccoli florets

handful of mung bean sprouts

⅔ cup raw peanuts

1 tbsp black sesame seeds

For the marinade:

½–1 tsp grated fresh ginger

3 tbsp tamari

5 tbsp orange juice

2 tbsp lemon juice

1 tbsp agave syrup

2 tsp cold-pressed sesame oil

1 tbsp onion powder (see p.152)

pinch of cayenne pepper

For the cauliflower rice:

1 cauliflower

¼ bunch cilantro

1 tbsp tamari

squeeze of lemon juice

1 tbsp cold-pressed sesame oil

1 Remove the stem from the red pepper, seed it, and cut out the pith. Slice the pepper into thin strips. Peel the carrots, and shave them into strips using a thin peeler. Cut the snow pea pods lengthwise in half. Peel the onion and slice it finely. Put all the vegetables and half of the mung bean sprouts into a large bowl.

2 To make the marinade, put all the ingredients for the marinade into a bowl and whisk them together well. Add the marinade to the vegetables, and toss to combine. Cover the bowl with plastic wrap. Let marinate for 2–3 hours, stirring occasionally.

3 To make the cauliflower rice, core the cauliflower and break the head into florets. Chop the core finely. Pick the cilantro leaves and chop them finely. Place the cauliflower into a food processor. Process it on a low setting, using the pulse setting, if your machine has it, so as not to chop it too finely. The cauliflower should resemble grains of cooked rice. Add the tamari, lemon juice, oil, and cilantro, and toss gently to combine.

4 Divide the vegetables, the rest of the mung bean sprouts, and the cauliflower rice between the plates. Sprinkle the peanuts and sesame seeds on top, and serve.

TIP If you have a dehydrator, you can also spread the vegetables out on 2–3 dehydrating trays and dry them for 2 hours.

SWISS CHARD WRAPS

Wrapping finely chopped vegetables in a beautiful, large, leaf is an easy way to make a quick lunch. With a tasty dip or spread on the side, the wraps are turned into a feast in a jiffy. The wraps also make neat, tasty packages that can be taken with you to the office for lunch. This version is one of my favorites.

Makes 6 wraps ▪ Preparation time: 30 minutes

2 tbsp lemon juice

pinch of salt or
   1 tbsp tamari

1 tsp cold-pressed sesame
   oil or toasted sesame oil

6 large Swiss chard leaves

1 carrot

1 beet

1 piece (1in/2½cm) cucumber

1 piece (1in/2½cm) daikon radish
   or 4 medium radishes

1 piece (1in/2½cm) zucchini

½ avocado

1 celery stick

3 large brown mushrooms

2 scallions

1 small handful of alfalfa
   sprouts, or other
   kinds, to taste

tahini (see p.60)

You will also need:
6–12 toothpicks

1 Combine 2 cups water, lemon juice, salt or tamari, and sesame oil in a bowl. Soak the Swiss chard leaves in the liquid for 20 minutes to make them pliable.

2 In the meantime, peel the carrot and the beet. Slice the cucumber lengthwise in half and, using a spoon, scrape out the seeds. Coarsely grate the carrot, beet, cucumber, radish, and zucchini, or cut them julienne. Slice the avocado lengthwise in half, remove the pit, and peel the avocado. Cut the avocado flesh lengthwise into strips. Thinly slice the celery and mushrooms. Thinly slice the scallions, including the greens, lengthwise. In a large bowl, mix together the vegetables and the sprouts.

3 Lay out the Swiss chard leaves on kitchen towels and pat dry. Spread a layer of tahini on each leaf, and put some of the vegetable mixture in the middle, leaving an edge of 1–1½in (2½–4cm) all around. Fold the upper and lower edges over the filling. Roll up each leaf from the bottom to the top. Use toothpicks to hold the wraps together.

4 Put the wraps onto plates. Serve with an extra bowl of tahini (see p.60), for dipping.

MUSHROOM CARPACCIO

These marinated brown mushrooms taste unexpectedly smoky and flavorful, almost reminiscent of bacon. This smoky flavor is sometimes missing when using white mushrooms. I like to slice the mushrooms quite thickly, which gives them a wonderful texture.

Serves 2–3 ▪ Preparation time: 20 minutes plus marinating

For the mushrooms:
1lb 2oz (500g) brown mushrooms
½ bunch chives
1 tbsp sesame seeds

For the marinade:
¼in (½cm) piece fresh ginger
½ red chili pepper (optional)
1–2 pinches of wasabi powder or 1 pea-sized dollop of paste from the tube
3 tbsp tamari
2 tbsp ume vinegar

1 Rub the mushrooms with a paper towel and slice them. Chop the chives. For a version that is not completely raw but enhances the flavor, lightly toast the sesame seeds in a frying pan without using any oil.

2 To make the marinade, peel the ginger and grate it finely. If using the chili pepper, remove the stem and slice finely. In a small bowl, mix together all the ingredients for the marinade and 1 tablespoon water.

3 Pour the marinade evenly over the mushroom slices and let the mushrooms marinate in the sauce for at least 30 minutes. Occasionally stir gently so that the marinade evenly covers all the mushrooms.

4 Arrange the mushrooms on a large plate in an overlapping, circular pattern. Sprinkle with the chives and sesame seeds, and serve.

TIP Ginger lovers can increase the amount of ginger a touch in this recipe. You can also try substituting paper-thin slices of beet or daikon radish for the mushrooms. If you do this, sprinkle the slices with cashew "cheese" (see p.99).

Savory & sweet
WILD RICE

Serves 4 ▪ Preparation time: 30 minutes plus soaking and drying

Although rice dishes truly aren't on the raw food menu, this dish is fantastic and a perfect balance between sweet and savory. Even though the soaking process takes a while, preparing this dish is essentially child's play, and even doable for someone with a very busy schedule. I have a lot of confidence in this recipe.

2 cups wild rice

4 celery sticks

7 scallions

2 carrots

2 bunches flat-leaf parsley

8 tbsp dried cranberries

3 tbsp onion powder (see p.152)

2 tbsp garlic powder

4 tbsp tamari

2 tbsp white-miso paste

2 tbsp ground chia seeds

2 persimmons

½ tsp paprika

salt and freshly ground black pepper

½ bunch dill

You will also need:

food dehydrator

1 Put the wild rice into a large bowl. Add 4 cups water, and soak the grains overnight. Then, put the bowl into the dehydrator to warm for about 24 hours at 104°F (40°C).

2 Drain the rice into a fine-meshed sieve. Rinse thoroughly under cold running water. Press the surface lightly to extract the excess moisture from the grains, and dry them on a kitchen towel.

3 Dice the celery finely. Coarsely chop the scallions, including the greens. Peel and grate the carrots. Pick the parsley leaves and chop them, but not too finely. Coarsely chop the cranberries.

4 In a large bowl, combine the wild rice, vegetables, cranberries, and the remaining ingredients (except for the persimmons, dill, paprika, and seasoning). Let stand briefly. Cut the stems off the persimmons and purée them in a food processor, or with an electric mixer. The purée should still be a bit chunky. Season to taste with the paprika, salt, and pepper. Chop the dill finely.

5 Divide the rice dish between the plates and sprinkle with dill. Serve the puréed persimmon on the side.

TIP "Cooking" rice also works without a dehydrator; it just takes longer. Soak 1 cup of rice in 3 cups or, even better, 4 cups of water for about 3 days, or until the grains of rice have become soft. Change the water twice daily. As soon as the grains have swollen, change the water again, and put the rice in the fridge until you are ready to use it. Sometimes when the rice grains expand, they look like the blossoms of an exotic plant.

*QUINOA
COUSCOUS

This is an uncomplicated, lovely dish, especially if you enjoy chopping. The photo shows the quick version, but the dish tastes even more delicious when the ingredients are finely chopped.

Serves 3–4 ▪ Preparation time: 20 minutes plus soaking

1 cup quinoa
1 small red onion
1 medium red pepper
1 medium yellow bell pepper
1 tomato
½ cucumber
½ bunch mint,
    or 2 tbsp dried mint
½ bunch flat-leaf parsley
½ cup black olives, pitted
2 tbsp cold-pressed olive oil
1 tsp sea salt
3–4 lemon wedges, to serve

1 Soak the quinoa overnight in plenty of water. Drain the water just before using. Pat the kernels dry with a paper towel. Peel the onion and slice it finely. Remove the stems from the peppers, seed them, and cut out the pith. Remove the stem from the tomato. Leave the cucumber unpeeled. Finely dice all the vegetables. Pick the mint and the parsley leaves, and chop. Slice the olives in half, or dice them finely.

2 In a large bowl, carefully toss the onion, vegetables, and olives together with the chopped herbs, quinoa, olive oil, and salt. Let stand briefly to marinate. Serve with the lemon wedges.

TIP I love to serve quinoa couscous with a lemon wedge and a dollop of coconut yogurt (see p.25), which is something that I always have in the fridge. A spoonful of pickled onion goes really well with it, too! And, for a Moroccan touch, just stir in a few raisins.

SWEET POTATO CURRY *with buckwheat*

Serves 3–4 ▪ Preparation time: 30 minutes plus soaking and chilling

This makes a very lovely, colorful lunch. I soak the buckwheat overnight. If you want to use sprouted buckwheat, this needs to soak for a little longer. In this dish, I love to vary the type of oil I use since this immediately changes the flavor. At the moment, I'm enjoying using truffle oil, which is not to everyone's taste. I find it goes very well with sweet potatoes and carrots.

For the curry:

1¼ cups raw or sprouted buckwheat groats

4 tbsp walnut oil

salt and freshly ground black pepper

3 large sweet potatoes

2 large carrots

¾in (2cm) piece of fresh ginger

bunch of cilantro

handful of peas (frozen)

1 tsp curry powder

1 lemon

pinch of cayenne pepper

1 tbsp black sesame seeds

For the sauce:

1½ cups cashews

2 tbsp lemon juice

1 tbsp curry powder

1 tsp salt

1 Put the buckwheat and the cashews for the sauce into separate bowls. Soak them overnight in cold water. Drain them just before using. If you are using sprouted buckwheat, rinse it in a sieve under cold running water, and pat dry. Season with 2 tablespoons of oil and a bit of salt and pepper.

2 To make the sauce, place the cashews, lemon juice, curry powder, and salt into a food processor. Process until the sauce is really creamy and has no cashew clumps. Carefully add water, one tablespoon at a time, until the sauce has the desired consistency.

3 Peel the sweet potatoes and carrots. Grate them coarsely. Peel the ginger, and grate it finely. Pick the cilantro leaves and chop them coarsely. Put the sweet potatoes, carrots, cilantro, and the defrosted peas in a bowl. Add the rest of the oil and the curry powder, and combine. Fold in the buckwheat and the curry sauce. Juice the lemon. Season the curry with the lemon juice and the cayenne pepper. Marinate the curry in the refrigerator for 1 hour before serving.

4 Sprinkle the sweet potato curry with the sesame seeds, and serve.

TIP This is a very versatile basic sauce. For example, you can use it as a marinade for thinly sliced carrots; by adding a little less water, you can turn it into a spread; or use it as a layer in wraps, under the vegetables.

PARSNIP & SWEET POTATO PURÉE

Serves 2–3 ▪ Preparation time: 20 minutes

This purée goes really well with mushroom carpaccio (see p.107). Although the flavors of the two dishes are very different, they complement each other in a very interesting way.

¾ **cup macadamia nuts**

1–2 **sweet potatoes**

1–2 **parsnips**

3 **tbsp almond milk (see p.148)**

1 **tbsp cold-pressed olive oil**

1 **garlic clove**

½ **tsp ground cumin**

pinch of freshly grated nutmeg

½–1 **tsp sea salt**

freshly ground black pepper

1 Place the macadamia nuts into a food processor or, even better, a coffee grinder, and grind them as finely as possible. Peel the sweet potatoes and the parsnips and dice them finely.

2 Place all the dry ingredients into a food processor and process until creamy. Slowly add the almond milk. If you need more liquid, you can add up to ½ cup water. Lastly, add the olive oil, the peeled and finely grated garlic, the spices, and seasoning.

TIP The amount of liquid you will need to add to make a lovely, creamy purée depends on the quality and condition of the ingredients used.

Mushroom, parsnip & KOHLRABI RICE

Serves 2–3 ▪ Preparation time: 20 minutes

This is one of the easiest quick recipes to make when I need a rice substitute. I use it as a side dish, wrapped in nori sheets, instead of using sushi rice, on salad, or as a quick snack with a bit of tamari and cilantro or mint. The mushrooms lend a smoky flavor, the parsnip a bit of sweetness, and the kohlrabi a pleasing freshness. This dish tastes best when it is fresh.

¼ **bunch flat-leaf parsley**

¼ **bunch cilantro**

1 **kohlrabi**

1 **parsnip**

1 **large handful of white mushrooms**

salt

1–2 **tsp tamari (optional)**

1 Pick the herbs, and chop them. Peel the kohlrabi and parsnip, and chop them into large pieces. Place the kohlrabi into a food processor, and process on a low setting. Use the pulse setting, if your machine has it, so as not to chop the vegetable too finely. It should resemble grains of cooked rice. Repeat this step with the mushrooms.

2 Stir in the parsley and cilantro, and season the mixture with salt. If the rice needs a bit more flavor, add tamari just a teaspoonful at a time, taking care that the rice does not become too moist.

KALE CHIPS

Makes 1 large bowl of each kind ▪ Preparation time: 20 minutes each kind plus drying

Once you have tried this absolutely fantastic substitute for potato chips, you will never again be tempted to devour a plate of humdrum potato chips! Kale is becoming very popular in the US and England, so much so that it's available year-round. New Yorkers, especially, are crazy about it. "Kale chips" are available everywhere, it seems, and they are made by countless companies in a huge variety of flavors. Here are a few of my favorites, which I created along with my friend Lisa. My favorite kind are the sweet kale chips. Lisa doesn't even wait to put the kale in a dehydrator but likes to eat it with the dressing as a salad right there and then, which is also good. But we want to make chips, after all ....

1lb 10oz (750g) kale

For the Japanese chips:

2–3 tbsp lemon juice

1 tbsp white-miso paste

2 tbsp agave syrup

1½ tbsp cold-pressed olive oil

1 tbsp tamari

½–1 tsp sea salt

For the Indian chips:

**4 tbsp cashew paste
(see p.148)**

2 tbsp agave syrup

2 tbsp lime juice

2 tbsp liquid coconut oil

1–2 tbsp cold-pressed olive oil

½ tsp ginger powder

2 tsp curry powder

1 tsp garam masala

pinch of cayenne pepper

1 tsp sea salt

For the Hungarian chips:

4 tbsp cashew paste

6 tbsp apple cider vinegar

4 tbsp cold-pressed olive oil

1 tsp sweet paprika

1 tsp sea salt

For the sweet chips:

1 banana

5 tbsp agave syrup or maple syrup

4 tbsp cashew paste

4 tbsp liquid coconut oil

1 tsp pure vanilla extract

pinch of salt

You will also need:

5–6 dehydrating trays with ventilating holes

food dehydrator

1 Clean the kale, cut out the thick ribs, and tear or cut the leaves into bite-size pieces.

2 To prepare each kind of savory kale chips, put the kale and all the other ingredients into a large bowl, and toss. To prepare the sweet kale chips, first mash the banana. Purée the banana and the remaining ingredients in a food processor, or use an electric mixer. Massage the mixture into the kale leaves.

3 Spread out the kale on dehydrating trays that have ventilating holes. (This is very important.) Dry the kale in a dehydrator at 104°F (40°C) for 5–7 hours. The drying time will depend on the dehydrator. Test for crispness occasionally.

TIP The number of dehydrating trays you will need depends a bit on the size of your pieces of kale. Make sure to spread out the pieces in one layer, and leave room between the pieces: if the pieces of kale are too close together, the kale chips will not become crispy.

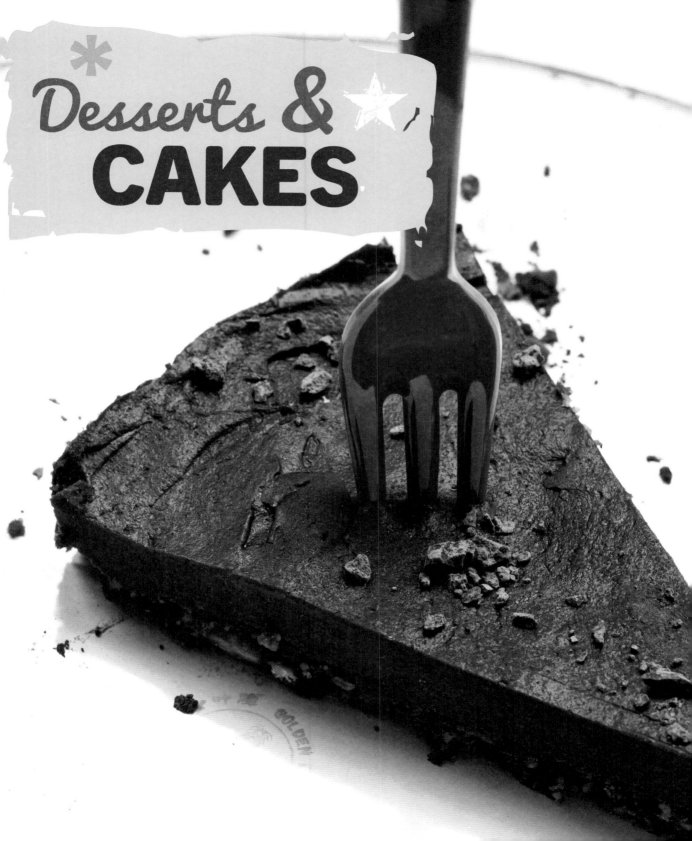

Desserts & CAKES

SWEET THINGS

Healthy but sinful calories

Raw desserts consist of much more than just chopped-up fruit. The question "How can anyone make cake and tortes without baking?" is a natural one. I can promise you though that you don't have to bake in order to make cake, as you will see. With a bit of creativity, tortes that will impress your guests can be made from nuts, dried fruit, and products made from cocoa or coconut. And have you ever considered serving cake half-frozen? If not, it is high time you did!

Seen from a nutritional standpoint, a raw food dessert is certainly much healthier than its cooked counterpart. (I have to smile when I think about regular versus uncooked desserts, as to me, raw desserts are every bit as delicious.) Unfortunately, I must disillusion all those who believe that they can eat a large slice of raw food torte without suffering any regrets. Because even though raw food desserts are extremely rich in nutrients, the number of calories they contain is barely distinguishable from those in regular, non-raw-food desserts—the raw food torte definitely will not become a diet dessert. In any case, raw food desserts are extremely filling, so much so that you are unlikely to overindulge in them.

THIS IS WHAT'S IN THEM—THE "BAKING" INGREDIENTS

Desserts in this chapter contain coconut oil, cocoa butter, and raw cocoa powder. Avocados lend a creamy consistency and also have a relatively neutral flavor (just in case you were wondering what on earth avocados are doing in desserts). Dates are also often used. They provide a balanced sweetness and are often found in cake bases, since they keep the "dough" together nicely. Dates are, so to speak, the "gluten" of raw food. For the best results, I recommend using the medjool date. This has a wonderful, soft consistency and definitely has a more intense flavor than most other kinds of dates. If you use smaller and drier fruits, it is best to soak them in water for 2–3 hours before using them, as this makes them softer and easier to work with.

Heavenly raw food desserts

The Rocher torte (see p.139) was the catalyst of a truly "historic moment" for my raw food era began after I had enjoyed a slice. Previously, I had virtuously drunk my green smoothies and rather dispiritedly chewed on dried fruit. A friend brought me a piece of this cake from the vegan supermarket around the corner. After the first bite, I thought, "It can't really be possible that THIS is raw food!" By the time I ate the last forkful, I was already determined to discover who had created this fabulous cake and to learn, right away, everything needed to create such grandiose desserts myself. The rest is history. A week later, Lisa Müller was standing in my kitchen, and today I am still learning so much from her amazing talent for creating delicious raw food desserts. The Key lime pie recipe (see p.136) also comes from her, and it has long become one of my standards. Thank you, Lisa!

* FRUIT PAPER

Fruit paper is the perfect snack when I have a hankering for something sweet. Usually, I prepare this recipe without adding any sweetener, since the sweetness of the fruit is more than enough.

2 mangoes

2 organic limes

1 lemon

4–5 ripe bananas

pinch of ground cinnamon

1 pineapple

small handful of fresh
    mint leaves

You will also need:

1–2 dehydrating trays

food dehydrator

**Makes 3–4 dehydrating films ▪ Preparation time:
10 minutes plus dehydration**

1 Peel the mangoes and cut the flesh from the pits. Zest and juice the limes. Place the mango flesh and the lime zest and juice into a blender. Purée on the highest setting for 2–3 minutes.

2 Juice the lemon. Peel the bananas and break them up into pieces. Place them into the blender, add the lemon juice and cinnamon, and purée.

3 Peel and core the pineapple. Place the pineapple into the blender, add the mint, and purée.

4 Spread the three fruit purées evenly and thinly (about the thickness of a coin) on three separate dehydrating trays. Place the trays in the food dehydrator and dry at 104°F (40°C) for about 5–6 hours. When you can peel the "paper" easily from the trays, turn over the leaves of fruit purée and leave them in the dehydrator for another 1–2 hours.

5 Remove the dried fruit paper from the trays and, using a clean pair of kitchen scissors, cut them into the desired shapes.

TIP Stored in an airtight container or jar, the fruit paper will keep for several weeks.

* DECADENT
STRAWBERRIES

Serves 4 ▪ Preparation time: 25 minutes plus resting

I make these chocolate strawberries for my son as an alternative to his beloved sugary snacks. But this is also one of my favorite recipes to make when friends call ahead to say they are dropping by and I want to serve them something a little sophisticated. Strawberries dipped in chocolate always have had something a bit magical about them, I believe.

2 tbsp coconut oil

2 heaped tbsp cocoa powder

drop of vanilla extract

**3 level tsp lucuma powder
or 1 tbsp agave syrup**

pinch of Himalayan salt

1lb 2oz (500g) strawberries

1 Melt the coconut oil over a water bath. Add the cocoa powder, vanilla extract, and lucuma powder or agave syrup to the oil, and stir to combine. Add the Himalayan salt.

2 Rinse the strawberries and dry them thoroughly. Leave on the hulls, which make convenient dipping handles. Dip the lower half of each strawberry into the liquid chocolate mixture. Place the strawberries on a baking sheet lined with parchment paper and refrigerate. Let the chocolate harden for 5–10 minutes. If you would like a thicker layer of chocolate, keep the chocolate warm and dip the strawberries into it again, then return to the refrigerator.

TIP The lucuma powder gives the chocolate a caramel-like, healthy sweetness, which is why the recipe doesn't need any other kind of sweetener. You can, of course, use other kinds of fruit, such as bananas or blueberries. I thread the blueberries on toothpicks, leaving some of the toothpick free at the top to dip them in the chocolate with and to pick them up with afterward.

*PERSIMMON *pudding with* CASHEW CREAM

The delicious cashew cream goes well with many things besides this unique take on persimmon pudding. You can use it as a topping for a variety of other desserts, muesli, or fruit salad. Unfortunately, it keeps for only about 3 days, so I simply whip up a small portion just when I need some. It would be too enticing to always have in the fridge!

Serves 3–4 ▪ Preparation time: 15 minutes plus soaking

For the cashew cream:

⅔ **cup cashews**

1 tsp lemon juice

1 tsp maple syrup or 1 date (medjool date is best)

drop of vanilla extract

For the pudding:

4–6 ripe persimmons

pinch of ground chipotle powder or cayenne pepper

1 tbsp sesame seeds

1 Soak the cashews overnight in cold water. Drain just before using them.

2 Place the cashews, lemon juice, maple syrup or date, vanilla extract, and ½ cup water into a blender. Purée on the highest setting for 3–5 minutes.

3 To make the pudding, remove the stems from the persimmons and cut the fruit into large cubes. Sprinkle the chipotle powder or cayenne pepper and the sesame seeds over the persimmon. Enjoy immediately. Serve the cashew cream on the side.

TIP This cashew cream recipe has been kept deliberately plain so that it can accompany many other dishes. You can, of course, adapt it by adding cinnamon, rose water, fennel, or other interesting spices.

PEANUT BUTTER BALLS
in chocolate

Serves 3–4 ▪ Preparation time: 30 minutes plus soaking and chilling

Salting the peanuts here provides a nice contrast to the sweetness of the chocolate. If you have ever tried "peanut butter cups," you will know what I mean. You can leave the ground peanuts just as they are if you like, or sweeten them with agave syrup. More authentic— and, in my opinion, better—is the variation that uses salt only.

For the peanut butter balls:
1¼ cups raw peanuts
salt
1–2 tbsp agave syrup
1½ tbsp coconut oil, plus a little extra for oiling the hands

For the chocolate coating:
2 tbsp coconut oil
2 heaped tbsp cocoa powder
3 level tsp lucuma powder or 1 tbsp agave syrup
pinch of Himalayan salt
drop of vanilla extract

1 Soak the peanuts overnight in cold water. Shortly before using, drain them in a sieve and pat them dry.

2 Place the peanuts into a food processor and purée until you have a fine paste. This calls for a bit of patience since it can sometimes take up to 10 minutes, so don't give up. Stop the machine occasionally to scrape down the sides. Season with salt and agave syrup.

3 Melt the coconut oil over a warm water bath and add it to the puréed peanuts. Process until well combined. Refrigerate the peanut butter mixture for 30 minutes to harden. The coconut oil ensures that the mixture will bind quite quickly.

4 To make the chocolate coating, melt the coconut oil over a warm water bath. Put the cocoa powder and lucuma powder or agave syrup into a bowl. Add the oil. Stir to combine. Whisk in the salt and vanilla. Oil your hands with coconut oil and form balls the size of walnuts from the peanut butter mixture. Dip the balls into the chocolate and place them on parchment paper to dry. Once the chocolate has hardened, you can repeat this step a second or even a third time, to taste.

5 Serve the peanut butter balls for dessert. They also make a tasty snack.

TIP You can refine this treat even more. When you have finished dipping the balls into the chocolate and the chocolate has not yet completely hardened, roll them in coconut flakes, chopped dried goji berries, cacao nibs, or cocoa powder.

*Chia & CAROB pudding with MANGO TOPPING

Serves 2 ▪ Preparation time: 15 minutes plus soaking

With a bit of luck, from September onward, you might be able to get ahold of fresh carob pods, also known as locust pods, in a specialty store or online. Along with the chia seeds, the fresh or ground carob seeds provide excellent nutritional value, as well as adding a very special flavor to this dessert. This recipe is so easy that even my 8-year-old son can make it on his own. He loves to see how the chia seeds quadruple in size after soaking. Even adults are surprised at the look and consistency of this dish. This is a perfect dessert with a fun factor!

For the pudding:

4 tbsp chia seeds

1 cup coconut water

7 tbsp carob powder (see tip)

2–3 drops vanilla extract

1 tsp raisins or chopped dates

For the topping:

1 mango

1 tbsp coconut oil

drop of vanilla extract

1 Put the chia seeds and the coconut water into a large bowl. Set aside to soak for 30 minutes, stirring occasionally so the seeds do not clump together.

2 In the meantime, make the topping. Peel the mango and cut the flesh from the pit. Melt the coconut oil over a warm water bath. Place the mango, coconut oil, and vanilla into a powerful blender or food processor and purée them on the highest setting for 2–3 minutes.

3 Stir the carob powder and drops of vanilla extract into the chia and coconut water mixture. Stir in the raisins or chopped dates.

4 Divide the pudding between small bowls or dessert glasses and top with the mango purée. You can also serve the purée on the side, if you wish.

TIP You can easily make carob powder yourself from carob seed pods. Using a sharp, pointed knife, slit each pod along one side and open it out. Remove the hard seeds. Put them into a food processor and grind them on the highest setting for 3–4 minutes into a powder. Stored in an airtight container in the refrigerator, the powder will keep for at least 1 week. It tastes really good sprinkled over muesli.

CHOCOLATE CHIP MINT *mousse*

Serves 4 ▪ Preparation time: 10 minutes plus chilling

Peppermint makes this mousse very refreshing. Not only the mint, but also the spirulina powder, give it its bright green color. This is a genuine summer dessert! Spirulina algae is considered the best source of protein in raw food cooking. Quite a few vegans (as well as astronauts!) use spirulina powder daily as a nutritional supplement.

4 dates (medjool are best)

2 cups thick almond milk (see tip)

1 tbsp almond paste

5 tbsp coconut butter or coconut paste

2 tbsp cocoa butter

1 tbsp spirulina powder, plus a little extra, to serve

4 tbsp dried peppermint leaves

1 tbsp vanilla extract

1 heaped tbsp cocoa powder

pinch of salt

3 tbsp maple syrup or agave syrup

1 tbsp cacao nibs, plus a little extra, to serve

You will also need:

nut milk bag

1 Pit the dates. Place them into a powerful blender. Add the remaining ingredients, except for the cacao nibs, and purée. Pour the mixture into a bowl. Stir in the cacao nibs.

2 Divide the chocolate chip mint mousse between 4 dessert bowls. Refrigerate for 2–3 hours before serving. Sprinkle with cacao nibs and a touch of spirulina powder, to serve.

TIP The almond milk used in this dessert is a bit thicker and fattier than regular almond milk, which helps the mousse ingredients to bind better. To make it, soak 1 cup almonds in cold water overnight. Drain the almonds just before using them. Place the almonds and 1½ cups water into a powerful blender or food processor. Purée on the highest setting for 2–3 minutes. Strain the mixture through a nut milk bag.

This dessert is amazingly easy to prepare. And by using a ring mold, you quickly transform this healthy dessert into a dish that is worthy of haute cuisine!

* APPLE CRUMBLE
with vanilla sauce

Serves 2–3 ▪ Preparation time: 30 minutes plus soaking

For the vanilla sauce:
⅔ cup cashews
juice of ½ lemon
1 tbsp maple syrup
¼ tsp vanilla extract

For the apples:
4 apples
1 tbsp maple syrup
juice of ½ lemon
1 tsp vanilla extract
½ tsp ground cinnamon

For the crumble:
1¼ cups almonds and
    pecans, mixed
2 tbsp date paste (see p.60),
    plus a bit extra, to serve

You will also need:
2 appetizer ring molds

1 Soak the cashews overnight in cold water. Drain them just before using.

2 Cut the apples into quarters, remove the cores, and cut them into a medium dice. Gently toss together the apples, maple syrup, lemon juice, vanilla extract, and cinnamon, and leave to marinate for 20 minutes.

3 In the meantime, make the crumble. Coarsely grind the almonds and pecans in a food processor or a mini food processor. Add the date paste and process until well combined.

4 To make the vanilla sauce, put the cashews, lemon juice, maple syrup, vanilla extract, and 3 tbsp water into a powerful blender. Purée for 3–5 minutes on the highest setting.

5 Place the appetizer ring molds on dessert plates, fill them half-full with the marinated apples, and press down firmly on the apples. Fill the top halves of the rings with the crumble, and press down lightly on the mixture.

6 Carefully remove the metal molds. Decorate each apple crumble with a few spoonfuls of vanilla sauce and a bit of the date paste, and serve.

TIP During the holidays, make a more wintry version of this by adding some pumpkin pie spice or gingerbread spice to the crumble.

This recipe was developed by my friend Lisa. Although I actually prefer to stick to quick recipes, this version of the classic Key lime pie is so good that I don't mind spending a bit longer in the kitchen. I now have made this pie countless times for parties and birthdays. Preparing the pie is really easy; it just takes time to prepare all the ingredients.

For the base:

2 cups cashews

1¼ cups shredded coconut

pinch of salt

1¼ cups dates (medjool are best)

1 tbsp coconut oil

For the topping:

¾ cup cashews

3 large avocados

5 organic Key limes

½ cup agave syrup

½ cup birch sugar (xylitol)

pinch of salt

¾ cup coconut oil

You will also need:

10in (26cm) springform cake pan

parchment paper

Key LIME PIE

Makes 1 10in (26cm) cake, or 14–16 pieces ▪ Preparation time: 45 minutes plus soaking and chilling

1 Soak the cashews overnight in cold water.

2 To make the base, place the cashews for the base into a food processor and chop them to make a course flour. Add the shredded coconut and salt. Remove the pits from the dates and add them. Pour in the liquid coconut oil (see tip, p.139), and process the ingredients. Line the pan with parchment paper. Press the dough evenly into the pan, and refrigerate.

3 To make the topping, drain the soaked cashews and rinse them well. Slice the avocados in half, remove the pits, and scoop out the avocado flesh. Grate the zest of two Key limes and juice them. Place the cashews, avocados, lime zest, and lime juice in the blender or food processor. Add the remaining ingredients, except for the coconut oil. Process until thick and creamy. Slowly pour in the coconut oil and mix to combine. Pour the mixture over the base. Put the cake in the freezer for at least 2–3 hours.

TIP You can serve the Key lime pie either half-frozen or, if you prefer it softer, defrosted. Delicious!

When we recently made a Rocher torte, there was leftover topping. My friend Irina had a lovely idea for using it up. We simply spread it on crackers and bread instead of commercial hazelnut and chocolate spread! To get that special nougat taste, you can bend the 100 percent raw food rule a little. Just toast the hazelnuts in a frying pan, without using any oil, before chopping them.

*ROCHER TORTE

Makes 1 10in (26cm) torte, or 14–16 pieces ▪ Preparation time: 1 hour plus chilling

For the top layer:
¾ cup cashews
¾ cup hazelnut paste (see p.148)
⅓ cup maple syrup
⅔ cup birch sugar (xylitol)
⅔ cup cocoa powder
pinch of salt
¼ cup coconut oil
⅓ cup cocoa butter

For the base layer:
1½ cups hazelnuts
1 cup cacao nibs
pinch of salt
8 dates (medjool are best)
2 tbsp coconut nectar

For the topping:
½ cup hazelnuts
⅓ cup cacao nibs
2 tbsp birch sugar (xylitol)
pinch of salt

You will also need:
10in (26cm) round springform cake pan
parchment paper

1 Soak the cashews overnight in cold water. Drain them just before using.

2 To make the base layer, place the hazelnuts, cacao nibs, and salt into a food processor, and process to make a coarse flour. Pit the dates, add the coconut nectar, and mix everything until the nuts have combined with the other ingredients.

3 Line the pan with parchment paper. Press the dough evenly into the pan. Put the pan in the refrigerator.

4 To make the top layer, rinse the soaked cashews well. Place them into the food processor and add the remaining ingredients, except for the coconut oil and cocoa butter. Purée until thick and creamy. Melt the coconut oil and cocoa butter (see tip), add them to the mixture, and process to combine. Pour the mixture into the cake pan, even out the surface, and chill for 2 hours in the freezer.

5 To make the topping, place all the ingredients in a food processor and chop them coarsely. Sprinkle them over the torte before serving. The torte will keep for about 5 days in the refrigerator, or up to a month in the freezer.

TIP Cocoa butter and coconut oil can be melted in a water bath. But in winter, when I only need a small amount of melted cocoa butter or coconut oil, I put the butter or oil in a small screw-top jar, or a very small pan, and set it on the radiator for a short time to melt.

Raspberry CHEESECAKE

Makes 1 10in (26cm) cheesecake, or 14–16 pieces ▪ Preparation time: 45 minutes plus chilling

For the base:

⅔ cup cashews

¾ cup pecans

¾ cup walnuts

3 tbsp chia seeds

⅔ cup dried cranberries

pinch of sea salt

For the filling:

2¾ cups cashews

¼ cup coconut oil

4 tbsp cocoa butter

6 tbsp lemon juice

½ cup agave syrup

¼ cup maple syrup

1 tbsp vanilla extract

For the topping:

⅔ cup frozen raspberries

1 cup frozen strawberries

3 dates (medjool are best)

½ cup dried cranberries

zest of an organic orange

3–4 fresh mint leaves

You will also need:

10in (26cm) springform cake pan

aluminum foil

1 Soak the cashews for the base (⅔ cup) and for the filling (2¾ cups) overnight in cold water. Just before using them, drain them and pat them dry.

2 To make the cheesecake base, place the pecans and walnuts in a food processor and process to a coarse flour. Add the ⅔ cup of cashews and grind them briefly. Then, add the remaining ingredients and process. Line the base of a springform cake pan with aluminum foil. Press the dough evenly into the pan, then refrigerate.

3 In the meantime, make the filling. Melt the coconut oil and cocoa butter (see tip, p.139) and pour them into a blender. Add the rest of the cashews and the remaining ingredients, and purée. If the mixture is too thick, add water, but only a few drops at a time. Spread the filling over the chilled base and put the cheesecake into the freezer for 1 hour.

4 Place the ingredients for the topping into the blender, setting aside a few perfect raspberries to decorate. Purée on a low setting for just 1–2 minutes so the mixture does not become too runny. Spread the topping over the chilled filling. Using a fork or a finger, score the surface of the topping lightly so that the light filling can be seen through the topping, creating a marbled effect. Sprinkle the remaining raspberries on top, and put the cheesecake in the freezer for 45 minutes to set.

5 Take the raspberry cheesecake out of the freezer for about 30 minutes before serving to defrost a bit. Serve the cheesecake half-frozen.

APPLE SLIVERS
with almond cream

For 1 ▪ Preparation time: 10 minutes

This is a lovely, uncomplicated dessert, and so simple to make. The apple slivers make a quick breakfast if you don't feel like a smoothie one morning.

For the almond cream:
⅔ cup almonds
1 date (medjool are best)
drop of vanilla extract

For the apple:
1–2 apples (such as Braeburn)
1 tsp sesame seeds
1–2 tbsp white or black
    chia seeds
squeeze of lemon juice
1 tsp maple syrup, plus a bit
    extra, to serve
½ tsp ground cinnamon
drop of vanilla extract
pinch of salt

You will also need:
nut milk bag

1 To make the almond cream, soak the almonds overnight in cold water. Drain them before using.

2 To make the apple salad, cut the apples into quarters, core them, and grate them coarsely with the peel still on. To add flavor, roast the sesame seeds in a frying pan without using any oil (but then the recipe is no longer completely raw). Add the sesame seeds, chia seeds, lemon juice, maple syrup, cinnamon, vanilla extract, and salt to the grated apple, and toss. Leave the apples to marinate for a few minutes.

3 In the meantime, for the cream, put the almonds, 1 cup water, the pitted date, and the vanilla extract into a blender. Blend on the highest setting for 2–3 minutes. Strain the liquid through a nut milk bag.

4 Place the apple sliver mixture on the plate. Serve the almond cream and a bit of maple syrup in separate little bowls on the side.

TIP Keep the almond pulp left in the nut milk bag in the refrigerator to add to muesli. You can also make almond flour from the pulp by drying the pulp in a food dehydrator or oven. Depending on the dehydrator, this will take 4–6 hours at 104°F (40°C). It is great to know that you can turn a by-product into something as yummy as cookies, for example. This is true alchemy!

CHOCOLATE

CHIP *cookies*

Makes 12 ▪ Preparation time: 20 minutes plus chilling

Here is my absolute favorite cookie recipe. The original version was created by Ani Phyo, an American raw food expert. I love her recipes! I have baked her cookie recipe at least a hundred times, tweaking it a bit more each time. I finally stuck with this version, because I find it the most delicious.

**small handful of unsweetened
dried mandarin oranges**

1 organic lime

**1½ cups almond flour
(see p.143)**

**½ cup almond paste
(see tip, p.148)**

3 tbsp cacao nibs

4 tbsp dried cranberries

1 tsp poppy seeds

3 tbsp agave syrup

**1–2 tsp pure vanilla
extract or the seeds of
2 vanilla beans**

½ tsp ground ginger

½ tsp dried rosemary

¼ tsp sea salt

1 Grind the dried mandarin oranges in a mortar. Finely grate the zest of the lime.

2 Transfer all the ingredients to a large bowl. Using your hands, mix everything together thoroughly. Dip a tablespoon into water. Drop the dough in tablespoons onto a sheet lined with parchment paper. Press down gently on each portion to flatten it a little. Put the cookies into the refrigerator for 1 hour to harden.

TIP Other dried and coarsely grated citrus fruits can be used, if dried mandarin oranges are not available. Peel the fruit, cut it into thin slices, and dry it in a food dehydrator at 104°F (40°C) for 7–8 hours. An added bonus—the whole kitchen smells of the citrus fruit.

BROWNIES

This was my first homemade raw food dessert. As though it were yesterday, I can remember how nervous I was that the recipe might not work out, and how amazed I felt when I saw how easy it was. There are endless fabulous brownie variations, and some are more complicated than this. But the aim here is to make delicious treats with the least possible effort, and this is the perfect recipe for doing so!

For the dough:

5 dates (medjool are best)

½ cup almonds

¾ cup walnuts

⅔ cup pecans

3 tbsp agave syrup

4 tbsp cocoa powder

¼ tsp vanilla extract

For the topping:

1 tbsp plus 1 tsp liquid coconut oil

3 tbsp coconut butter

4 tbsp cocoa powder

1 tbsp cacao nibs

3–4 tbsp coconut sugar or birch sugar (xylitol)

You will also need:

6 × 8in (15 × 20cm) baking pan

Makes 1 pan, 6 × 8in (15 × 20cm), or 12 pieces ▪ Preparation time: 40 minutes plus soaking time and chilling

1 Soak the dates overnight in cold water. This intensifies their sweetness. Drain just before using them. Pit the dates.

2 Chop the almonds in a food processor, then add the walnuts and pecans, and chop. Add the remaining dough ingredients and process until smooth and combined. Don't worry if you can see a few pieces of nuts, as this will make the brownies nice and crunchy.

3 Using your hands, press the dough evenly into the cake pan. It should be about 1in (3cm) high. Put the brownies in the refrigerator for 30 minutes to harden.

4 To make the topping, melt the coconut oil and coconut butter (see tip, p.139). Place them into a blender, add the remaining ingredients, and blend until everything is well combined. If needed, carefully add a bit of water—the mixture should not be too runny. Spread the topping over the brownie dough. Put the brownies into the refrigerator for 30 minutes for a final chill, or into the freezer for 10–15 minutes.

5 Cut the brownies into large pieces. They will keep in the refrigerator for 4–5 days (if they survive that long without being eaten).

TIP You really should soak dates for several hours if you don't use medjool dates. Also, the dough might not be sweet enough if you use other kinds of dates. If you do use a different date, add a bit more agave syrup or coconut sugar for added sweetness. I like a bit of fruit in my brownies, and sometimes I add a small handful of dried cranberries, cut in half, to the ingredients.

Basic recipes
ALMOND MILK

Makes 1 quart ▪ Preparation time: 5 minutes plus soaking

1 cup almonds
or other nuts
½ vanilla bean
1 tsp agave syrup
pinch of sea salt

You will also need:
nut milk bag

1 Soak the almonds overnight in cold water. Scrape out the vanilla bean. Just before using, drain the almonds. Place them into a powerful blender or food processor. Add the vanilla, agave syrup, sea salt, and 1 quart cool water, and purée very finely.

2 Pour the mixture into a nut milk bag and, using your hands, squeeze out the liquid.

TIP Don't throw away the very fine almond pulp left in the nut bag. Spread it on a baking sheet to dry. The result—gluten-free almond flour.

NUT PASTE

Preparation time: 5 minutes plus soaking

2 cups nuts
(almonds, hazelnuts,
or cashews)
2 tbsp neutral oil

1 Nut paste is very easy to make yourself. Soak the nuts overnight in water. Just before making the nut paste, drain the nuts and put them into a powerful blender or food processor. Add the neutral oil and purée the nuts, starting on the middle setting, then increasing the speed to the highest setting until smooth.

2 Kept in a screw-top jar, the paste will keep in the refrigerator for 6–7 days.

RAW FOOD *Kitchen tips*

Germinating and growing sprouts

Using pea sprouts as an example, soak the peas overnight in cold water. Drain before using. Put the peas into a sprouter or germinating jar. Water two to three times a day. If you use a sprouter, open the level containing the peas occasionally to air, since gases can develop. At normal room temperature (70°F–75°F/21°C–24°C), the pea sprouts will be ready to harvest after germinating for 3–4 days. Organic peas are best.

Juices and smoothies

I am not a huge fan of freshly squeezed juices. They are delicious, of course, but from a nutritional standpoint, I think they are inferior to smoothies. However, they are useful for detoxifying the body or for a juice cleanse.

Few of us, including me, own a really good juicer (see p.154) that can handle greens well and deal with the fibers. But you can indirectly juice greens in a blender. All you need is a fine-meshed sieve to strain out the fibers; a smoothie without fibers is pure juice.

Melting cocoa butter and coconut oil

If I need only a small quantity of liquid fat, I use my easy winter method to melt these. I put the still-solid fat into a screw-top jar, or in a small pan, and set it on the radiator. The fat melts in no time while I am doing other things.

Soaking water of dried fruit and dried tomatoes

Don't discard the water you have soaked dried fruit in. You can use it in blended drinks and in sauces instead of plain water. This often saves adding additional sweetener. Dried tomato soaking water keeps very well in the fridge for a few days. Whenever you need to thin a liquid, this is often a good alternative to water. It also adds flavor!

Soaking nuts and seeds

Many dishes call for nuts and kernels that have been soaked before using them. This makes them easier to digest and frees their enzymes. Just remember always to rinse soaked nuts, seeds, and pulses, too, before using them.

Toasting grains and kernels

If you are very strict about following raw food diet guidelines, you should not toast nuts and seeds, since they are heated to over 104°F (40°C). Here, because of the flavor, I make an exception.

Warming ingredients and foods

As an alternative to warming food gently in dehydrators, you can also warm your food in the oven. To keep your oven temperature at about 104°F (40°C), turn on the oven light and stick a wooden spoon in the oven door to keep it open a crack. The temperature might reach about 113°F (45°C). Since ovens vary, use an oven thermometer to check the temperature of yours.

RAW FOOD INGREDIENTS

To follow a raw food diet, you must always use cold-pressed oils. Any nuts, seeds, and dried fruits you use should be dried at low temperatures. You definitely can integrate fermented products into your diet, such as sauerkraut, miso, or soy sauce. Just make sure, when you purchase them, that they are of raw food quality.

Agave syrup, also known as agave nectar, is a sweetener made from the agave plant. In vegan and raw food cuisine, it is used as a substitute for honey. Compared to honey, it is more fluid and sweeter. It is available in supermarkets and health-food stores. However, new research has shown that it is no healthier than sugar, so high-quality maple syrup is preferable.

Almond flour, also known as almond meal, is made from ground almonds. It contains valuable mineral nutrients such as magnesium, iron, fluoride, and potassium, as well as B-vitamins and vitamin E. It gives baked goods a nutty flavor. You can also make almond flour yourself from the pulp that is left over from making almond milk (see tip, p.143).

Almond paste of raw food quality is made from raw almonds. It provides many important mineral nutrients and vitamins, especially magnesium, B-vitamins, and vitamin E. It can be used as a spread, but also gives a subtle almond flavor to sauces, dressings, and desserts. Almond paste (see p.148) is available in health-food stores or stores that sell organic products, but is also very easy to make yourself.

Arame *see* seaweed.

Birch sugar (xylitol) is not an exotic raw food product, but a healthy alternative to sugar. Although it is industrially processed, birch sugar has many excellent qualities, among them that it does not raise the blood sugar level much and helps to fight cavities. You can purchase it in health-food stores, in some pharmacies, and online.

Cacao nibs are made from cocoa beans. They are made by breaking shelled cocoa beans into small pieces. Cocoa beans have the highest concentration of antioxidants of all foods. Cacao nibs can be used as an ingredient in almost all dishes, such as smoothies, desserts, chocolate, and ice cream. They can also be ground into cocoa powder.

Carob is the fruit of the carob tree (also known as the locust tree). This long, brown, dry-looking pulse is a wonderful ingredient in desserts. Carob is low in fat and rich in fiber, and it is said to promote calorie burning. Carob powder is available practically everywhere as a substitute for cocoa. I avoid it, since the industrially processed powder has a strong bitter taste and, apart from its color, does not have very much in common with drinking chocolate. The fruit of the carob tree, carob seed pods, are not all that well known in some countries, which means you will have to do a bit of hunting to find them. Your best bet is in fine food stores, Asian grocery stores, or online. If you are lucky enough to find carob pods, try them out (see tip, p.130)!

Carob flour is a gluten-free, neutral-tasting binding ingredient made from the seeds of the carob tree.

Celery salt, a fantastic, aromatic salt substitute, can be made easily in a food dehydrator. Dice 2–3 celery sticks and dry them in a food dehydrator for 5–10 hours (depending on the make). Then pulverize the dried celery in a coffee grinder or a powerful blender.

Chia seeds are often called a "superfood." The small seeds, which come from Latin and South America, are, in comparison to other seeds, immensely rich in protein. Their calcium content exceeds that of milk fivefold. Chia is also an enormous source of omega-3.

Chipotle powder adds spice to many hearty dishes and goes very well with kelp noodles, for example. It is made from smoked jalapeño peppers. It is hard to tell whether or not the chilies have been cold dry-smoked, because only then are they considered truly raw food. If you want to be sure, you can make ground chipotle powder yourself. There are instructions for how to do this online.

Cilantro juice If you don't have a slow juicer and can't juice herbs, check whether your local health-food store stocks this, or go online to find out where you can purchase this juice.

Cocoa powder tastes really good in nut-milk drinks, and it also gives desserts a chocolate taste. To make it, cacao nibs are ground and pressed to make cocoa butter and cakes of chocolate. The cakes are ground to make raw powder. In comparison to industrial cocoa powder, raw cocoa powder has a slightly higher fat content.

Coconut butter is not refined, deodorized, hardened, or bleached and has a wonderful coconut flavor. Since coconut butter is cold-pressed, it contains important enzymes, vitamins, and minerals and is a valuable dietary source. It is sold in health-food stores and in stores selling organic products.

Coconut cream is made from the meat of young coconuts. It has many uses in the kitchen. It gives a light coconut flavor to desserts, but also can be used for flavoring sauces and curries. It is available in health-food stores, in stores that sell organic products, and online.

Coconut nectar, also called coconut sugar, tastes a bit like caramel and can be used as a sweetener. Also, coconut nectar has a very high ORAC value, which is a measure for the concentration of antioxidants. Thickened, dried, and ground, it becomes coconut sugar (see below).

Coconut sugar contains many antioxidants and mineral nutrients. Compared with many other types of sugar, especially refined industrial sugar, it is low on the glycemic index. You can purchase it in health-food stores and in stores that sell organic products.

Coconut water, the pure water from young coconuts, is not only low in fat and calories, but also very healthy due to its high mineral content. Unfortunately, it is not all that easy to find young coconuts. Packaged coconut water is, by comparison, now readily available. But since it is pasteurized, it doesn't conform to raw food criteria.

Dates should be soaked in water for around 2 hours before using them, but not longer, since otherwise too much of their sweetness will seep into the water. You don't have to soak medjool dates in water. These are the softest and sweetest dates on the market.

Date paste is one of the most versatile sweeteners in raw food cuisine. At the same time, it provides flavor and texture. Date paste is an ingredient that I always have in the fridge. It is very easy to make it yourself. See page 60 for the recipe.

Dried tomatoes are something you always should have in your pantry. Check the list of ingredients when you buy dried tomatoes. It should only list tomatoes and, at most, salt. When you make them yourself using a food dehydrator—this is really easy and takes about 8 hours—you know for sure what is in them.

Glass noodles, also called bean-thread or cellophane noodles, are made from mung bean starch and widely used in Asian cooking. They are available in every well-stocked supermarket and in Asian grocery stores. Make sure when buying them that they are made only from mung beans and that no potato starch or other, similar additives have been used. Glass noodles are easy to digest and have a low glycemic index. Since they are flavorless, they make a good platform for other flavors. I prepare glass noodles by pouring hot water over them, but I can live with this.

Ground flaxseed is also known as flaxseed meal. It is made from the cakes formed by pressing flaxseed to make flaxseed oil. It contains important omega-3 fatty acids, is rich in vegetable protein and fiber, has neither carbohydrates nor sugar, and also is gluten-free. It helps bind baked goods. You can purchase ground flaxseed in health-food stores or online. You also can make the flour yourself by grinding to flour whole flaxseed in a coffee grinder or a powerful blender on the highest setting.

Hazelnut paste in raw food quality, is made from raw hazelnut kernels, and cold-pressed without any additives. It gives sauces, dressings, and desserts a nutty flavor. You can buy it in health-food stores, in stores that sell organic products, or online. You can also make it yourself in no time using a powerful blender. See page 148 for the recipe.

Honey is not permitted in a strict raw food diet since it comes from living creatures. But I am glad to make an exception here.

Kefir culture powder is fairly common in the raw food diet and provides raw food eaters with a nutritional component. Since the powder consists of probiotic bacteria, it is not, strictly speaking, a raw food ingredient. It turns homemade coconut milk into kefir, which keeps for up to 10 days in the refrigerator.

Kelp noodles have relatively little flavor, go with everything, and are very versatile. Their texture is comparable to that of glass noodles. Kelp is an algae and is therefore an excellent source of iodine and other micronutrients. *See also* seaweed.

Lucuma powder is very nutritious and rich in beta-carotene, vitamins, and minerals. The fruit the powder is made from grows in the mountains of Peru. I like to use it as a sweetener, since it has a caramel-like flavor and gives dishes a better texture. It is probably easiest to purchase it online.

Maca powder, a nutritional supplement with a slightly floury taste, is made from the root of the maca plant, which belongs to the watercress family. It contains protein; a great deal of iron, zinc, and important mineral nutrients; as well as almost all vitamins, making this root a real energy powerhouse. It has an effect similar to ginseng. Maca powder tastes good in all desserts and smoothies, but also in soups and sauces. You can purchase it online.

Miso paste can be used as a substitute for salt and should be used judiciously. This tangy soy paste is produced by using bacteria and yeast to ferment soybeans, salt, and grain (rice or barley). The process

can take months or years. The darker the miso paste is, the stronger the flavor.

Nori sheets are sheets made from nori, a type of seaweed. Nori is an indispensable source of protein for those on a raw food diet. *See also* seaweed.

Nut pulp is a by-product produced when you make nut milks such as almond milk. It is much too valuable to simply throw away. You can make crispbread (see p.29) from it, or dry the pulp and grind it to make flour.

Oils can only be considered to have raw food quality if they are cold-pressed. This is usually indicated on the label. There is often information about the producers of raw-food-quality oils on their web pages.

Onion powder is something you should make yourself in order to ensure raw food quality. To make it, peel an onion and slice it very thinly using a food slicer or a sharp knife. Put the onion slices into a food dehydrator and dry them at 104°F (40°C) until they are completely dry. Alternatively, turn on the oven light and dry the onion slices on a baking sheet lined with parchment paper. This takes about 6–7 hours. Leave a wooden spoon in the oven door so that the moisture can escape. Then grind the dried onion in a mortar or a blender to powder and store it in an airtight container.

Parsley juice For those of you who don't have a slow juicer and can't juice herbs, parsley juice is sold in some pharmacies. It isn't, strictly speaking, a raw food since it is heated briefly during production to kill bacteria and lengthen its shelf life.

Piri-piri is a small West African chili that is often sold as a powder made from the ground pods or in paste form. In Africa and the Mediterranean area, it is universally used and added to all dishes that need some spicy heat.

Purslane is a valuable source of vitamin B12. Its tart and salty taste makes it a very special wild vegetable, but you will have to do a bit of research to find out who sells it. It can often be found at organic-food stores and in fine food stores.

Salt is something of which we consume too much. I have observed that salting food has become, for many, almost a reflex action. You should try to break this habit if possible. In general, you should take care not to use industrially refined salts, but instead use good-quality unrefined salts, such as Himalayan salt or Celtic sea salt.

Seaweed, which is sold dried, is wonderful in raw food cuisine. It is much loved in Japanese cuisine, but also in many European countries. Of all the many kinds, I use arame, nori, and wakame seaweed most. It is important to note that, since seaweed is rich in iodine, you should eat no more than 1½ tbsp daily. Dried seaweed is available in some supermarkets, organic-food stores, and Asian food stores.

Sesame seeds are a popular ingredient in Middle Eastern, Greek, and Turkish cuisine. Sesame oil is indispensable in Asian cuisine. I like it not only for its abundance of nutrients—such as manganese, calcium, and magnesium—but also for its flavor, and therefore use it frequently. Sesame seeds can be purchased as white or black seeds—the darker the color, the stronger the flavor.

Spirulina powder is made from a type of algae. It is a nutritional supplement and is rich in protein and vitamin B12. Spirulina is sold in powder and tablet form. It is thought to bolster the immune system, help mitigate allergic reactions, and even improve energy levels. You can buy it in organic supermarkets, health-food stores, and online.

Sumac has a tart, bitter taste and lends a fruity flavor to many dishes. To make this spice, which originated in the eastern Mediterranean area, the red fruit of the sumac is dried and coarsely ground. Sumac is sold in many fine food stores and supermarkets, as well as in Asian supermarkets and online.

Takuan is rich in vitamin C and is a traditional Japanese staple food. It is made from daikon radish that first is air-dried and then fermented. Takuan has a subtle salty-sour taste. As it ferments, it turns yellow. Takuan can be purchased in organic stores, Asian stores, or in online stores selling macrobiotic products.

Tamari is made by fermenting soybeans, sea salt, and water. It is a gluten-free alternative to naturally fermented soy sauce, which contains added wheat. It is a very versatile seasoning, and widely available.

Ume vinegar, also called ume plum vinegar, or ume su, has a lovely sour, fruity flavor. This salty Japanese seasoning sauce is a by-product created during the processing of Umeboshi apricots. It can be used in the kitchen just like vinegar and goes with many dishes.

Wakame *see* seaweed.

Zahtar is a spice mix made from sumac (see this page), sesame seeds, the zahtar herb, and salt. It is very popular in North Africa, the Middle East, and Turkey, where it traditionally is mixed with oil and brushed over flat breads, such as pita. But it also seasons dishes and dips of all kinds just as well. You can buy zahtar in many regular supermarkets, speciality supermarkets, or online.

USEFUL *Kitchen aids*

Appetizer ring molds

Ring molds are usually made of stainless steel and come both in round and square shapes. They are used to form food into elegant shapes before serving. They make even the simplest of dishes magically look like haute cuisine.

Blender

For raw food cuisine, it is important to have a powerful blender that has at least a 750-watt motor—or, even better, 1,100–1,200 watts. You can, of course, also use a food processor.

Coffee grinder

For grinding and shredding small quantities of ingredients, an electric or hand-powered coffee grinder is an excellent alternative to a food processor.

Dehydrating trays

These trays or sheets are the parchment paper of dehydrators. Depending on the manufacturer, the trays are also called paraflexx sheets or teflex sheets. They come with and without holes and are nonstick. This makes it easy to peel fragile fruit paper (see p.123), thin crackers, or chips (see p.116) from them.

Food dehydrator

A food dehydrator is indispensable for a varied raw food diet. Dehydrators are not exactly cheap, but the investment pays off. You not only can dry fruit in it, you can also make raw food baked goods. Spread on dehydrating trays, fruit purées turn into delicious fruit paper (see p.123). When buying one, check to make sure that the dehydrator has a powerful fan so that food dries evenly. Good dehydrators allow you to set the temperature between 86°F (30°C) and 158°F (70°C). Raw food quality is achieved by drying food up to 104°F (40°C).

Food processor

When you purchase a food processor, look for one that also slices, grates, and rasps, and can process even small quantities well.

Grater

To coarsely or finely grate garlic, ginger, and vegetables of all kinds, you need a sharp hand grater. They are readily available.

Juicer

You can make your own juice from almost every kind of firm fruit and vegetable with a good juicer. Using a high-quality "slow juicer," you can even juice herbs. Unfortunately, these machines are quite expensive, but there are now some centrifugal juicers in the midprice range that are very efficient.

Nut milk bag

Nut milk bags are used to separate the "milk" of nuts that have been soaked and puréed in a blender from the pulp. They are made of high-quality synthetic material, such as nylon, and are better than sieves since you can squeeze the bags. A cheap alternative is to repurpose mesh laundry bags—the kind you can buy to wash your delicates in—as nut milk bags.

Seed sprouter

For those who want to grow their own sprouts, it is best to use a seed sprouter. There are many kinds and many manufacturers.

Spiralizer

A spiralizer is a vegetable slicer that cuts vegetables into spirals. It is a must-have tool for every raw food lover. It turns many kinds of vegetables into spaghetti-shaped spirals in no time. The simplest and cheapest models look like huge pencil sharpeners. If you plan on using yours often, it pays to buy a larger model that adheres to your work surface with suction cups.

Vegetable peelers

There are so many excellent hand-held peelers on the market now, and they make easy work of preparing your vegetables. Peelers with swivel blades, also called thin peelers, take away the least peel and are good for shaving vegetables into thin slices.

Vegetable slicer

A vegetable slicer is the best and simplest tool for cutting vegetables into really thin, even slices. My favorite slicer is a mandolin. The stainless-steel model might be more expensive than a plastic model, but it lasts almost forever, so buying one pays off.

TIP Many raw food ingredients are available in health-food stores, organic-food stores, or in very well-stocked supermarkets. And almost everything is available online, too.

INDEX

THANK *you!*

The fact that you are now holding this book in your hands seems to me to be almost a miracle. After searching unsuccessfully for a good raw food book in German, I once again did what I usually do with all my creations. If I don't find something that I like, I have to make it myself! And this is exactly how the idea for this book came about. Of course, between having an idea and realizing it, there are quite a few steps to take, and there are many wonderful people I met during the journey who supported me with their competence, engagement, and love!

First comes my friend and photographer Brigitte Sporrer, with her great talent and her unflappable nature, who would first photograph a dish and then calmly eat it for lunch. My dear Buffi, we both know everything we have gone through together, especially during photo production ;-)! Just this then—thank you for your friendship!

Also, I would like to thank Monika Schlitzer and Gabriele Kalmbach for their belief in this project and their sensitivity toward the subject matter. To me, they are true pioneers! Given her patience and understanding, Ulrike Kraus, my editor and email friend, made it easy for me to give my text a common thread!

The team also deserves a huge thank you—in particular, Sascha of "Raw Living," who, as the best online source for the raw food lifestyle, made sure all important ingredients were on hand for me and made them quickly and readily available. This is so important—please continue in the same way and never go out of business!

And thank you, dear Irina, for your little moments of cheekiness at the right time—and, of course, for your perfect organization during production.

Lisa, you know that without you, there would be no real raw food in my life. I love you!

And Linas, wherever you find yourself right now in the world (probably somewhere between San Francisco and the North Pole), thank you for everything that you taught me and for the best nights spent steamily cooking up a storm in the kitchen that I ever have had. Two maniacs at work!

A big fat kiss to my dear Gruchen. Wherever you are, inspiration is in the air ... and there is always room for me. For this, I thank you. Always. This is also true for you, Tutu. How could I write a book without mentioning you?

Thanks to my son Lilien for being the harshest critic of my green smoothies and always encouraging me to try out new creations. You know I love you more than anything. You bring sunlight to my heart, even when it's raining outside!

And last but not least, thanks to my mother. Although I no longer eat "vadas," your incomparable Hungarian beef dish, you are still the best!

For this edition

Translator Barbara Hopkinson
Editor Claire Cross
US editor Kayla Dugger
Editorial assistant Poppy Blakiston Houston
Senior art editor Glenda Fisher
Senior producer, pre-production Tony Phipps
Producer Samantha Cross
Managing editor Stephanie Farrow
Managing art editor Christine Keilty

DK Germany

Publisher Monika Schlitzer
Managing editor Gabriele Kalmbach
Production manager Dorothee Whittaker
Production coordinator Claudia Rode
Production Kim Weghorn

Recipes and foodstyling Anat Fritz
Photography Brigitte Sporrer
Editorial and text Ulrike Kraus
Graphic design, typography, and production Silke Klemt
Repro Medienservice Farbsatz

First American Edition, 2019
Published in the United States by DK Publishing
1450 Broadway, Suite 801, New York, NY 10018

Copyright © 2019 Dorling Kindersley Limited
Text copyright © 2014 Anat Fritz
DK, a Division of Penguin Random House LLC
19 20 21 22 23 10 9 8 7 6 5 4 3 2 1

001–314137–Jun/2019

A catalog record for this book
is available from the Library of Congress.

ISBN 978-1-4654-8402-4

DK books are available at special discounts when purchased
in bulk for sales promotions, premiums, fund-raising, or
educational use. For details, contact: DK Publishing Special
Markets, 345 Hudson Street, New York, New York 10014
SpecialSales@dk.com

Printed and bound in China

A WORLD OF IDEAS:
SEE ALL THERE IS TO KNOW

www.dk.com